THE SOUL'S COMPANION

Connecting with the Soul
Through Daily Meditations

TIAN DAYTON, PH.D.

Health Communications, Inc.®
Deerfield Beach, Florida

www.hci-online.com

©1995 Tian Dayton
ISBN 1-55874-358-8

Publisher: Health Communications, Inc.
            3201 S.W. 15th Street
            Deerfield Beach, Florida 33442-8190

Cover design by Linda Golden.

To Marina
to take with you
to college

I love you with all my
heart and soul

Mom

INTRODUCTION

Spiritual Growth as a Process

Spiritual and personal growth is a process, it happens one day at a time. Each day we carve out a few minutes of quiet time in order to remove ourselves from the pressures and anxieties of everyday life, to calm down and tune in on the deeper pulse of living. When we do this on a regular basis, we build up a reservoir of inner quiet that we can draw on throughout our day. The daily readings in this book will help you to focus your mind. Our souls are waiting for us to know them and through them the soul that contains all life. No one can know soul for us. Soul discovery is our own brave and courageous voyage. We voyage on the waters of life the way Odysseus rode on the sea; taming fears and drives, resisting the temptation that would lead to self-destruction so that that we can ultimately arrive safely home. The ancient scriptures grappled with our most fundamental issues. They teach us how to live ethically with sanity, values and meaning so that we do not get lost. They help us, through story and metaphor, to face our weaknesses and conquer our fears so that we can eventually get out of our own way and allow the light of soul or spirit or God to shine through.

We can only solve our lives for today. We can only live well, be happy, make ends meet or do a job *for today*. Just for today we can do what would confound and immobilize us if we felt we had to do it forever. We can only live, do or be one day at a time. We should resolve, within ourselves, that we will live as well as we can *for today*. Asking more of ourselves is unfair, asking less is unwise. *Just for today* is our best path out of yesterday, into tomorrow and for living in the presence of soul energy.

Soul, Self-Esteem and Health

Being lost can also be seen as being tied up in

destructive patterns of thinking, feeling, and behavior, engaged in a compulsive or neurotic relationship with living. Negative self-thoughts can lead to a negative self-image and conversely positive self-thoughts can help to build a positive self-image. The way that we think about ourselves or the inner dialogue that we carry on within our own minds can become a self-fulfilling prophecy. Describing this is a theory called "brain set." A person with a positive brain set will train her mind to identify life circumstances that support that positive set, that is, she will be quick to identify and value those experiences that are helpful and support her positive set. She will see as lucky what another person may not read as such. A person with a negative brain set will be quick to notice and take in those experiences that will match it. Research now shows us that visualizing positive experiences in the mind over and over again can actually elevate our T-cell, T-helper/T-suppressor cell ratio, thus strengthening the immune system, our first line of defense against disease. Daily readings, quiet time, journaling or sharing ourselves in trusting, supportive groups are proven tools for strengthening our physical, emotional and mental health.

How to Use This Book

1. As a daily reading to center yourself, quiet down and focus your mind.

2. As a warmup to your own personal journaling (see instructions on journaling on the next page or consult *The Quiet Voice of Soul* for exercises.)

3. As inspiration for writing your own daily affirmation, to help you to begin your own personal affirmations book, side by side with this one.

Methods

In a quiet moment, center yourself and read an affirmation in this book. You may wish to go in order of dates or just let the book open to any page and see what that page has to say to you. Allow whatever feelings that the reading brings up to come into your present moment. Sit with the feelings, observe the thoughts and simply be with them or, if you choose, use one of the following techniques to further explore them.

- Journal in the first person keeping pen to paper and allow your feelings to flow freely and fully onto the page. Try to write with as little break as possible.

- Journal in the third person describing the situation, e.g., she was 17, her name was Julie and she felt lonely on that hot summer afternoon, etc.
- Reverse roles with yourself at any time in your life and journal from or as that self in the first or third person, e.g., I am 12-years-old. My name is Roger and when I look around me I see, etc. You will be surprised at how much will emerge.
- Find a picture that speaks to you and write a monologue imagining what you're saying inside yourself from the point of view of the you in the picture, e.g., I am Lucy and I love to wear my hair like this. I am holding my mommy's hand, etc.
- Find a picture of someone else with whom you have strong feelings or unfinished business, reverse roles with them, and journal as that person (what you imagine they're feeling).
- Imagine someone with whom you have unfinished business and reverse roles with them. Speaking as them, describe yourself from their point of view, through their eyes (e.g., My name is Harry and I want to tell you something about my daughter Connie.)

- Write a fantasy biography of your life—not the way it was but the way it felt (e.g., I am a little frog who lives in a tiny room in a very big house, etc.)
- Name three blocks on your path toward soul. Reverse roles with any or all blocks you feel drawn into and write a monologue as that block (e.g., I am anger, I am endless, powerful and overwhelm Rita's life, etc.)
- Reverse roles with your mother and write a journal entry describing you. (e.g., I am Betty and I am describing Daniel, he seems to me, etc.) Repeat process with father.
- Write a letter to a person who you feel you've lost but still have much to say to that has remained unspoken. (This letter is for your own purpose, speak freely, fully. It is not for mailing.)
- Write a letter of forgiveness, asking someone you feel you have hurt for their forgiveness or a letter you wish you would receive from someone who has hurt you asking you for your forgiveness. (Again, these letters are for your own benefit, not to send.)

- Write a letter to God saying any and all of what you might like to say including getting angry if you choose—freely express all of your deepest hidden feelings to God.
- Make a wish list for your life and write it down in a letter to God.
- Open up to God and tell God in a letter what you like best about yourself and what you are ashamed of.
- Describe to God in a letter how you would like your life to be, outline, for example, a five-year plan for your life.
- Write a letter to God describing what kind of relationships you would like to have in your life and describe how you would like your work life to look.

Remember, your journal is for you, it is your place to express your thoughts and feelings freely and fully. When you journal, ask the editor in you to take a nap, and allow your inner voice to come forward in a sincere, open and uncensored manner.

Change begins from within and then extends outward. Something from outside can stimulate it but until it happens inside of us, it's not ours. Deep, personal reflection can create a paradigm shift, a change in perception or a shift in the way we *see* both ourselves and our world. Viewing the world as alive with soul entails just such a shift in perception. A quiet, subtle shift with a profound, life-altering effect. It is your experience, a quiet happening in the privacy of your own soul. It is a process and happens one day at a time.

With warmest wishes for a full and happy life,

Tian Dayton

January

Listen to the Exhortation of the Dawn!
Look to this Day!
For it is Life, the very Life of Life.
In its brief course lie all the
Verities and Realities of your Existence;
The Bliss of Growth,
The Glory of Action,
The splendor of Beauty;
For Yesterday is but a Dream,
And Tomorrow is only a Vision:

But Today well lived makes
Every Yesterday a Dream of Happiness,
And every Tomorrow a Vision of Hope.
Look well therefore to this Day!
Such is the Salutation of the Dawn!

Sanskrit poem,
author unknown

Seeing Soul

Today I will see soul in the ordinary. Wishing, waiting and hoping for soul to be hand-delivered to me, tied up in a neat little ribbon, and read to me like a report will not bring me closer to my soul experience. I will discover soul in my day, I will allow it to surface and recognize it when it does. Soul is everywhere waiting for me to see it. I will cultivate this seeing as part of my personal discipline—looking past the surface, staying with what surrounds me until I feel it gently transform, become deeper, luminous, extraordinary. When I learn to really see soul in the ordinary, it will present itself to me. It will show me its true radiance. I will see what I have not seen and be surrounded by soul.

I will learn to see soul.

The World is too much with us . . .
Getting and spending, we lay waste our powers . . .
Little we see in Nature that is ours;
We have given our hearts away. . . .
For this, for everything, we are out of tune;
It moves us not—Great God!

William Wordsworth

Defining the Soul

I will not try to define the soul today. When I seek to categorize or give place to the soul, I lose contact with it. I connect with it through thought and definition rather than through sensing. Soul is experiential. These senses that I have, my sight, hearing, touching and so on, are what allow me to know the soul. I am alive and soul is alive; we are made of the same particle stuff, issuing from one source. There is no beginning and no end, no way to be separate from what is, no place that is not *the* place. Running after soul only makes it elude me—not because of the act of running, but because of seeing it as somewhere other than where I am.

I will seek direct experience of soul.

What stuff is soul made of? The question is as meaningless as asking what stuff citizenship or Wednesdays are made of. The soul is a holistic concept. It is not made of stuff at all. Where is the soul located? Nowhere. To talk of the soul as being in a place is as misconceived as trying to locate the number seven or Beethoven's 5th Symphony. Such concepts are not in space at all.

Paul Davies

Letting Soul Speak

Today I will let my soul speak. I will connect with that part of myself that sees through soulful eyes and senses the soul within the moment. There are no moments more beautiful than this one—the tree, the sky, the birds that sing their song from the treetops are waiting to be seen. The veil that lies over soul in the present moment is growing thinner as I sit in quiet and trust that soul is there. The soul I seek is already with me, within, without, never-ending, always alive—it is nothing more or less than life itself.

▼

I will take the time to
tune in on soul.

Affirmation of life is the spiritual act by which man ceases to live unreflectively and begins to devote himself to his life with reverence in order to raise it to its true value. To affirm life is to deepen, to make more inward, and to exact the will to live.

Albert Schweitzer

Passing Soul By

I will not pass soul by like a stranger in the night. I will look for it. I will be still and wait for the veil of illusion to be lifted so that I can see what is behind it. Soul is not locked in a jewel box or floating somewhere in the sky. It is not the province of a privileged few. Soul is there for me when I am ready to look, willing to embrace it and make it part of my day-to-day living. Soul is not obscure and oblique; it is simple—so simple that I pass it by without noticing its presence. Soul is quiet, so quiet that I do not hear it calling. There is no path toward soul, no journey or secret passageway that will lead me to it. Soul is here and now. It is present in all that is.

I am willing to see soul.

We only see the outer covering of reality and it's only when our inner senses are opened, when our inner life is opened, that we pierce through the unreality.

Sister Pascaline Coff

Clean and Wholesome Living

Today the quiet and abiding rhythm of a clean and wholesome life well lived are enough for me to be happy. I do not need one more extraordinary pleasure, another beautiful object or rare experience to tell me what I already know—that this world is alive and beautiful. The quiet pleasures of day-to-day living will reveal to me splendor enough. There is no need to create a perfect moment so that I can prove to myself that life is worthwhile. There are perfect moments happening all the time when I can learn to see them. When I learn to see soul in the ordinary, I will not need to wish, hope and dream for a moment of extreme pleasure to offset my sense of hopelessness. Hope and pleasure will be in front of me, surrounding me, within me. I will not deceive myself as to the whereabouts of soul. It is where it always was—everywhere.

I admire and appreciate the ordinary.

Unformed people delight in the gaudy and in novelty.
Cooked people delight in the ordinary.

Zen saying

Locating the Self

Today I give myself a rest in my frantic search for soul and self. If soul is present in all that is, how can I *find* it? I am both the finder and the found, the seer and all that is seen.

It is not easy to be with the moment and allow myself to experience deeper and deeper layers of reality; I am constantly tempted to get up, to lose myself in distraction. I continue to be involved with things that look like self, only to find soul is not contained there, either. I want to grab soul, hold it, put it away where I can't lose it again. I want to own it so that it cannot be taken from me. To accept that soul exists only in the moment-to-moment experience of life, and that it comes and goes with my awareness of it, can be difficult. It can make me want to bottle, store and label it. Today I will let soul go so that I can find it.

I will be present for soul and ask my soul
to be present for me.

How shall I grasp it? Do not grasp it. That which remains when there is no more grasping is the self.

Pandachari

The Face of Soul

The face of soul is the face of the person standing beside me. I will learn to see soul and God-nature in the people close to me. They are manifestations of the one eternal energy as surely as the sun or the stars. My own face carries spirit. Soul expresses itself through me; my hands, my face, my voice are the vehicles through which the spirit is made flesh. If I do not learn to see spirit here, then where will I look? Soul is not lodged in a building or suspended in circumstance. It is alive in the here and now. Soul cannot be relegated to any particular time or space. It is as potentially present in the marriage ceremony as in the ritual of mourning. If soul is anywhere, then it is everywhere. Turning my back on it in day-to-day living, then expecting it to be alive and well somewhere else, isn't how it works.

Soul is here and now.

Lift the stone and you will find me, cleave the wood and I am there.

Jesus

9

Organic Life

I am biologically programmed for development. Just as a flower grows from a seed, blooms, wilts and returns to the earth, I, too, have a life cycle. Dust to dust, ashes to ashes, I will come and go, be born, bloom and die. I am organic. I eat from the earth—I am a part of it, dependent on it. This is why I will love the world, because this world into which I am born is my spiritual and physical home.

I come from and will return to this world.

In the laboratory we can see daily things that come into existence and disappear, that pop into existence out of nowhere and then fade away. These are subatomic particles so it is all on a pretty small scale, but we can imagine that if we apply quantum physics to the universe as a whole, the entire thing, all the matter, energy and space could come into existence out of nowhere spontaneously as a gigantic quantum fluctuation. . . . Quantum physics' contribution is that of a universe that is not predetermined but an evolutionary pattern that is governed by probabilities, which creates a true openness.

Paul Davies

Real Living

Be with me, soul, live with me, know me, stay with me, invite me along your path of vision. Let me enjoy you and you enjoy me. We are one, you and I, like friends at the beach, like lovers in a glen, like a father and a child walking hand-in-hand, like a mother with her baby at her breast. Let me be with you. Let me wander through your thoughts and down the byways of your being. Let me breathe your breath and carry you securely within my heart, so that I will be alone no longer. Life without you is not life. Living outside of your presence is to be lost in a sea of ideas and objects, forms and shapes, without you there to give them meaning.

Let me be with soul.

There is no reality except the one contained within us. This is why so many people lead such an unreal life. They take the images outside them for reality and never allow the world within to assert itself.

Herman Hesse

▼

Playing

I will not look for soul today. I will not search or hack at the sediment that sits in its way. Today I will let soul chase after me—like children on a playground we will play tag, soul and I. I will hide in excited anticipation to be found and when I am, I will fuss and stamp my feet. I will whine and be a sore loser and then make up with soul, all to keep the game going—to keep it fun, lively and involving. But all the time, I will be easy to find. I will hide in obvious places and make noises. I will be a good playmate; the idea will be to keep playing—not to win or lose. Today I will take for granted that soul wants to be with me as much as I want to be with soul.

▼

I'm hiding—come find me.

To play is to be unfettered and unconditional, to perform actions that are intrinsically satisfying, to sing, dance and laugh. . . . As players, then the gods are revealed to be delightful, joyful, graceful beings whose actions are completely spontaneous, unconditional, and expressive of their transcendent completeness and freedom.

David R. Kinsley

▼

Soul in the Particular

Soul is present in all that exists; each particle of life contains soul and God-energy. Therefore, when I study the part, I am learning also about the whole. When I know the depths of my own mind I understand the minds of others. When I come to know the ins and outs of my own life pattern, I can use that knowledge to better understand other people's lives.

I am a blueprint of all that is. Each event carries layers of meaning. In penetrating the depths of any one subject, I am inevitably led toward the center. The center is the same, the paths vary. My job is to stay on course. It is my movement toward center that gives my life meaning and purpose. It is not the path that is crucial but my willingness to stay on it, to work through the blocks, twists and tangles I meet along the way. This is what produces inner growth and change, and brings me closer to soul.

▼

I will learn from the task at hand.

The more we understand individual things, the more we understand God.

Greek proverb

Creativity

Creativity is central to my experience of soul. It helps me to see evidence of soul in funny little nooks and crannies of living. It allows me to risk my own expression of self. Every act that I undertake can be made more beautiful when I allow my own creativity to shine through, to be at work in the mundane. Creativity is what can make the ordinary transform into the extraordinary. It is both a way of doing and of seeing, of behaving and of being. Whatever I do today, I will bring along my creative self. I will use day-to-day circumstances and events as a vehicle through which I allow my creative energies to flow.

I will experiment with life as an artist experiments with color. I will paint my own day. Events are my palette. My soul is my brush.

I will let the artist within me express itself.

Creative minds have always been known to survive any kind of bad training.

Anna Freud

Balance

Today I will have a balanced day. I will not be given to extremes either in action or in thought. Wide extremes of thinking, feeling and activity leave me sitting on the fringes, from where I have to find my way back in order to feel integrated. The edges are not good places to live. They make me feel stretched, taut and overly vulnerable. Living on the edges makes me think on the edges and behave in exaggerated ways. It leads me toward extremes in feeling and my reactions feel ungrounded, out of whack somehow because they are not coming from an integrated place within me. When soul is at my center and I choose to be centered in soul within me, I operate from a point of fullness and balance rather than a wobbly and empty place.

I balance within the soul in my own center.

Take calculated risks. That is quite different from being rash.

George Patton

I Am Ready

I will be ready. When death comes, I will understand that she has come for me. I am no exception, nor should I be. Along with all who are living, my case is terminal. A philosophy of life without a philosophy of death is not real, is incomplete, is blind to what we live with every moment in our unconscious. So much of me even now lives beyond my body, lives in something called soul. Why should the end of my body be the end of my soul? Why is it not just as logical to think my soul will go on forever? Both points of view are equally sane and equally mad. I will choose the one that best serves my living soul, my life today.

I choose life.

I have a dream that one day even the state of Mississippi, a state sweltering with the people's injustice, sweltering with the heat of oppression, will be transformed into an oasis of freedom and justice.
I have a dream that my four little children will one day live in a nation where they will not be judged by the color of their skin but by the contents of their character.

Martin Luther King, Jr.

Soul's Work Within Me

Today I will not develop soul, I will let soul develop me. I will open to its subtle lessons, and search out meaning in little things. Small coincidences and events will not escape my notice today. I will let soul come into me and invade my insides, cleanse and transform me and make me something I never dreamed I could be. Today I will trust the creative power of soul to exercise its artist's eye on all that I am, allowing its ingenuity, to move into what I thought I was and make it new. I will allow soul to transform me, and to do its spirited work on my inner depths.

I am in the vision of soul's creative mind.

They hear how
the artery of my soul has been severed
and soul is spurting out upon them,
bleeding on them,
messing up their clothes,
dirtying their shoes.
And God is filling me.

Ann Sexton

Living Daily with Soul

Do not forget about me today. Soul and I will not forget about you. Let us have our morning coffee together. Walk with me. When I speak, be in my words. When I think, shape my thoughts—act through me. Hold me steady throughout my day and keep me safe—safe from harm, safe from hate, safe from my own pettiness and blindness. Do not let me waste this day forgetting to be with you. I know that you are always present in the moment, waiting to be seen. Let me see you.

▼

I will not forget that soul is with me.

In the nineteenth century the problem was that God is dead; in the twentieth century the problem is that man is dead. In the nineteenth century inhumanity meant cruelty; in the twentieth century, it means schizoid self-alienation. The danger of the past was that men became slaves. The danger of the future is that men may become robots.

Erich Fromm

The I Experience

I am my own point of reference. All the life that surrounds me is integrated and experienced through this "I." I am like a transistor connected to radio waves. If I am clean and clear inside, I will get clearer messages. If I am lost in unfelt, unresolved emotional issues, my receivers will be impaired and I will not be in a position to get clear messages. I will tend to interpret experience in an overly subjective manner, seeing what goes on around me as either supporting or negating my position, and I will process experience through this colored lens.

Actually, there is no real path toward soul. When I sufficiently cleanse the self, soul is there. I will examine and work through the complex, dysfunctional patterns and traumas that the "I" has accumulated, so that I can be freer to experience soul.

I will see through a clearer lens.

Let your soul stand cool and composed before a million universes.

Walt Whitman

Being Available

Today I will invite the presence of soul. I will spend my day quietly preparing for soul to enter and when it does, I will notice it. I will notice soul energy as it seeps into my day, as it acts on the quality of an ordinary event, as it deepens and expands ordinary time. Making myself ready to receive soul is all I need to do. Bringing myself to center, breathing and quieting down will help bring me toward a state of mind that can experience soul energy. Today, I will make myself a welcoming vehicle for soul quality living.

I will wait for soul.

I ask all blessings,
I ask them with reverence,
of my mother the earth,
of the sky, moon, and sun my father.
I am old age the essence of life,
I am the source of all happiness.
All is peaceful, all is beauty,
all in harmony, all in joy.

Anonymous (Navaho, 19th-20th century)

Grief

Grief can be a teacher of the soul. It can temper me, it can open my eyes and heart to a wisdom and understanding borne from suffering. When I cannot grieve I carry wounds in silence. Grief can cleanse my psyche of frozen patterns—of complexes and compulsions held in place and hidden by unfelt pain. Feeling the pain that drives me into destructive forms of thinking and behaving can release the energy within me that has been stored and used to maintain rigid defenses. If I am willing to feel grief, then I don't have to defend against feeling it. All the energy I have used to keep from feeling pain can finally be freed. Grief is just a feeling and I will survive feeling it, knowing that it is only by experiencing it that I can let it go.

I am strong enough to feel real grief.

Let the young rain of tears come.
Let the calm hands of grief come.
It's not all as evil as you think.

Rolf Jacobson

The Moment

I will be quiet and experience the moment. When I accept that the day before me is a teacher, that it has within it as many of the deepest components of mystery, love and God as any moment of teaching or doctrine could contain, then to experience the moment is to experience the soul.

It is not that the search is not fascinating or exciting or even enlivening, only that there are no answers —at least, none based solely on intellectual belief systems. To seek the answers in those systems is to simply rearrange the question and find a partial answer. The experience of soul is the acceptance of the moment in which both the question and the answer dissolve and become irrelevant. I will allow myself to co-exist with soul energy, to become one with the moment and one with all that is contained within it.

I rest peacefully in the moment.

Experience of the eternal aspect in the temporal moment is the mythological experience.

Joseph Campbell

▼

Soul and Life

I accept the eternal nature of life. All that is alive is in a constant process of transformation; though something may seem to die, it is really just passing into another state. All that is alive issues from the same particle substance. Soul is present in all that lives. There is no separating my self from soul. Living with soul connects me with a transcendent reality. I am a part of eternity simply because I am a part of a living universe. If something dies, then everything dies. If life is eternal, then soul is also. Soul is life and life is soul.

▼
I choose life.

The stream flows,
The wind blows,
The cloud fleets,
The heart beats,
Nothing will die.
Nothing will die
All things will change
That's eternity.

Alfred, Lord Tennyson

▼

Walk Soft

Walk soft, my soul, and do not want what is not yours to have. Be strong and sturdy and accept what comes your way. Be grateful for all that is good in life and appreciate each day, the good that surrounds you. Do not let life embitter your soul within me—let it teach you and learn from it all you can. Love, every day love—for no noble reason. Love because it is better than not to love, and be kind to people who have less than you. Because if you have your soul, you have it all.

I have soul—I have all.

As the human species awakens to itself as a collection of immortal souls learning together, care for the environment and the earth will become a matter of the heart, the natural response of souls moving toward their full potential.

Gary Zukav

Shame

Today I will not let shame and guilt keep me from learning to live with love and soul in my life. If I let shame hold me back, I am letting darkness win. I will choose love whether I feel I deserve it or not. The shame and guilt that I may carry in secrecy need not isolate me from what is good. I will not hide my shame under more shame, or anger, or false vanity and pride. All I need to do is to acknowledge them and be willing to share this part of me with others, just as I share the side of myself that I feel good about. The more I am able to break the secrecy and the isolation of guilt and shame, the more it will lose its grip on me.

I will acknowledge all of me.

Love bade me welcome; yet my soul drew back,
Guilty of dust and sin
But quick-eyed love, observing me grow slack . . .
Drew nearer to me, sweetly questioning
If I lacked anything.

George Herbert

The Inner Physician

A calm and centered state of mind is not simply a nice attitude. It is a health-promoting clinic that exists within me. I need an overall life attitude that is health-promoting. I have a physician living within me. My body is like a laboratory that produces its own chemicals. The way that I think, feel and eat, the way I live my life, help shape the chemical makeup of my body. This affects my physical state of health.

I am a physical, mental and spiritual being.

Scientific findings have led the search for heart health into a new domain: that of the spirit. The new prescriptions include prayer, practicing forgiveness, going to church or temple, and surrendering to a divine authority. These developments beg the question: Is the heart merely a pump supported by an adequate flow of oxygenated blood and a steady supply of nutrients? Or is this fist-sized muscular organ the "seat of the soul," requiring nourishment on a spiritual level? If it is both, then what is the relationship between the physical and the metaphorical heart?

Henry Dreher

Balancing the Inner and the Outer World

I will not let the outside world overwhelm and obfuscate my inner world. When I was a child, I allowed my inner world to shine through. In growing up I grew away from my own insides. I split off from my inner being and put my energy into matching myself with what I saw around me, whether or not it was in accord with who I was, my own particular likes and dislikes. Eventually I lost contact with what I really thought and felt. I looked to others for confirmation and affirmation not because they were so interesting to me, but because I had silenced my own inner voice, sent my *self* into hiding. I didn't want anything to show that didn't *fit* in. I will worry less today about fitting in with the world and more about fitting the world within me.

I will listen to my own insides.

And the Lord God formed man of the dust of the ground, and breathed into his nostrils the breath of life; and man became a living being.

Genesis 2:7

Controlling the Outcome

I live with the illusion that if I try hard enough, think hard enough, work hard enough and plan well enough, I will be able to control the outcome of a given situation. Soul tells me to *take the action and let go of the results*. When I feel that I can control the outcome, I live in the result rather than the process. "Life is what happens when you are making other plans." Trying to control results dams up the waters within me. My energy is spent on managing rather than living. When I feel that I am somehow responsible for the outcome of a situation, I get tangled up in a tedious maze of micromanagement. I try to determine other people's feelings, perceptions and actions in an attempt to anticipate all the possibilities, so that I can better manage them. Living in the outcome is a way to avoid the present; consequently, it becomes living away from soul.

I take the action and let go of the results.

For this tiny little plant (the brain) is most in need of freedom, without which it goes to wrack and ruin without failure.

Albert Einstein

The Integrated Soul

I understand soul to be laced into the moment, a part of all that exists, a part of the particle mass from which all life flows, indivisible from life manifest and unmanifest. To try to isolate soul in order to pursue it relegates it to a thing apart, an experience waiting to happen. Soul is already present in all that exists. There is no need to break it off and chase after it. In fact, it cannot be separated—it can only be known and experienced in the here and now.

I allow soul to be.

Hinduism and Jainism agree that there is a continuing self, which is reborn. One of the important breaks made by the Buddha occurred at exactly this point. In his moment of great insight or enlightenment he suddenly realized that there is no self or soul hidden within the process. There is only the process itself, the continuous succession of moments in which the accumulation of what has constituted a life up to that moment gives rise to the next moment in succession.

J.W. Bowker

Self-Honesty

Understanding *how* I experienced certain life events gives me greater knowledge of myself and more detachment from my self-destructive patterns. When I refuse to remember the pain of early experiences—projecting it onto others and making it about them, rather than sitting with it and feeling it myself—rather than resolve the problem, I compound it. This is one way that I pass on pain through the generations. In my inability to sit with my own pain, I ask others to contain it for me through dynamics such as projection. It is identifying in someone else what I should be identifying in myself, displacing a painful feeling by dumping it onto an unsuspecting receiver. This does not allow me to do the inner work I require to be clean and healthy, and it crosses another person's boundary in an unfair, unhealthy way. My greatest potential for learning is in studying myself with honesty and openness.

I will look honestly at myself.

The wish for healing has ever been the half of health.

Seneca

▾

Living the Life That Suits Me

What I have to offer is unique, and the satisfaction of pursuing it is all I need for a soul growth experience. Soul in this sense is completely personal. It is my engagement with the process of self-expansion that develops soul and brings it into my day-to-day living. Years ago I had a friend who lived a somewhat nonconventional life, particularly for the times. When I pursued this with him, he said, "I go to a tailor to order a suit, instead of buying it off the rack so that I can get it to fit me perfectly. The arms are the right length. The shape suits my body and I choose the material and the cut that looks best on me. That's how I live my life. I tailor it to suit me. I live the life that fits me, that I can move about in easily, that feels the most comfortable."

Living the life that fits me, that is carefully tailored to my own personal inner form will, like a tailored jacket, last longer, wear out slower and look the best because it was designed especially for me.

▾

I tailor my life to my own shape.

The heaven of each is but what each desires.

Thomas Moore

31

A Communion of Subjects

All that is alive is subjective. When I look at life as a collection of inanimate objects, I disempower the moment, I reduce the process of living to navigating an obstacle course. Even if the objects are friends, they carry only a superficial, designated sort of meaning

For anything to be deep, it has to be alive. For anything to carry relevant meaning, it has to be interactive. For anything to have a soul, both the perceiver and the perceived must contain particles that are of the one particle, the one life, the one soul. Our minds can only go as deep as our world because we are contained within it. One mind, one soul, one particle.

I recognize the many contained in the one
and the one contained in the many.

The universe ultimately is a communion of subjects, not a collection of objects. . . . It's the deep mystery, the mystery of the sunset, the deep mystery of the stars at night, the mystery in the song of the birds, the waves of the sea, the mystery of the seagull. All these things carry the deep mystery of the universe.

Thomas Berry, *The Soul and the Universe*

The Observer

I will not pretend that I have access to a reality separate from the moment, that I am somehow detached and able to observe from a neutral, non-partisan position. Neutrality is only a matter of degree and can be an illusion. I am always a part of, a participant. Even the act of observing impacts and affects that which is observed. Just by being in a situation, even if I do not feel myself to be participating, I affect it.

I take responsibility for my effect.

The observer is part of the process so that we experience as well as experiment. You have a larger view of life if you have a scientific view of nature as well as a view of the machine of nature. (The purpose) is to live more fully, to perceive more fully instead of just studying nature. And, of course, at the end of the day it comes back to us because we are the observer, there's no one else. I can't look at the world in any other way than through my own eyes. So I'm part of what I'm looking at. Scientific objectivity in terms of looking away from ourselves at the external world is no longer viable. We are part of our own picture.

Richard Dixey, *The Soul and the Universe*

February

And a man said, Speak to us of Self-
 Knowledge.
And he answered, saying:
Your hearts know in silence the secrets of
 the days and the nights,
But your ears thirst for the sound of your
 heart's knowledge.
You would know in words that which you
 have always known in thought.
You would touch with your fingers the
 naked body of your dreams.

And it is well you should.
The hidden well-spring of your soul must
    needs rise and run murmuring to the
    sea;
And the treasure of your infinite depths
    would be revealed to your eyes.
But let there be no scales to weigh your
    unknown treasure;
And seek not the depth of your knowl-
    edge with staff or sounding line.
For self is a sea boundless and
    measureless.

Say not, "I have found the truth," but
    rather, "I have found a truth."
Say not, "I have found the path of the
    soul."
Say rather, "I have met the soul walking
    upon my path."
For the soul walks upon all paths.
The soul walks not upon a line, neither
    does it grow like a reed.
The soul unfolds itself, like a lotus of
    countless petals.

                        Kahlil Gibran

Combinatory Play

I will play with ideas. I will look at them from a variety of perspectives, examine them from all sorts of points of view. I will pull on them, test them, throw them up in the air and wait to see how they land. I will combine and recombine them, shuffle them and test them to see if they hold up under pressure. I will scatter them all over the floor and notice which parts of them leap out at me and which ones fade away. I will reinvent the wheel every so often just to stay in shape—just for the fun of it. I will use my mind and soul as a playground for ideas, my ideas. I will spin them like a top and let them go—throw them out like a boomerang and see if they will return. I will play.

I act as an incubator of ideas.

Einstein believed "combinatory play" to be . . . "the essential feature in productive thought—before there is any connection with logical construction and words or other kinds of signs which can be communicated to others." The underlying thesis here is that combinatory play leads to the "eventual establishment of a new perspective."

Christopher Bollas

FEBRUARY 2

Suffering

I will suffer. Suffering is a part of the human condition, a part of the growth of soul. When I run from it, I run from my potential to develop and awaken, to shed old, tired selves and be born into new ones. I could cling to the familiar, but it would make me become ridiculous and dead inside. After all, I change constantly. If I want to look forever young, for example, all I will accomplish will be to look like someone old who is trying to look young. I will be pathetic rather than beautiful.

Growth means change and change includes struggle. If I want to live and love fully, I will need to be willing to struggle. If I really care, I will be making myself vulnerable to hurt; but just for today I prefer that to walking through life unconscious and untouchable.

I see suffering as a potential for growth.

He who learns must suffer. And even in our sleep, pain that cannot forget falls drop by drop upon the heart, and in our own despair, against our will, comes wisdom to us by the awful grace of God.

Aeschylus

Self-Exploration

There is an ancient Chinese curse that says, "May all your wishes be granted." Like it or not, human beings seem to love a good struggle. So why deny it? Why fight the fight? At least if I am conscious of this quality, I can choose my battles rather than turning the situations that I care about most into battle-grounds. Ghandi was right when he said that the real battles in life are fought within. I need to look not only at where meaning can be found, but also where it cannot. I will explore those self-defeating beliefs, attitudes and behaviors that block my path toward soul. I will examine my walls of defense, take them apart brick by brick and see what they are made of. I will see what I am hanging on to and how I use my thought process to entangle rather than untangle my problems. I will live in the spontaneous moment of soul awareness.

I will learn from my mistakes.

Although the world is full of suffering, it is also full of the overcoming of it.

Helen Keller

An Empty Place Inside

I have an empty place inside, a God-shaped hole that seeks to be filled. This hole is meant to be filled with the energy and electricity of soul. If I do not fill it with soul, I will fill it with anything that is available, attempting to incorporate people and experiences within myself so that I will not feel empty.

Soul is present in people and activities. Allowing myself *to have the experience* that lies at my fingertips is a simple but profound path to soul growth. If soul is incorporated in all that lives, then all that lives is incorporated in soul, and inuring myself to the life that surrounds me inures me to my life within. Until these fears or holes are felt in the present moment, come to terms with and understood for what they are, I will not realize how near at hand the solution lies.

All that surrounds me is imbued with soul.

Earth's crammed with heaven
And every common bush afire with God:
but only he who sees takes off his shoes.

Elizabeth Barrett Browning

▼

The Shadow Self

Carl Jung described the shadow self as that part of ourselves that we attempt to deny—that we cast into the shadows of our own psyche or being.

The act of denying or hiding a quality from myself can actually strengthen it inside of me. There are also positive aspects of myself that I sit on, my unlived lives, or qualities that I wish to allow myself, but can't for some reason: something gets in the way of my free expression. When I don't allow myself these, I may feel jealous of someone who enjoys and expresses them because secretly I wish to do the same. Owning and exploring my own shadow requires that I be willing to know myself fully. When I deny parts of myself, I deny soul along with them because soul functions in all of me. When I bring my shadowy depths to a conscious level, I release the energy of my soul and my personality operates more efficiently and effectively.

▼

I am willing to open my eyes to me.

Knowing your darkness is the best method for dealing with the darkness of other people.

Carl Jung

Inner Guide

I have an inner teacher, an inner vision of who and what I can be. Coded into me is my own best self. Today I will consciously call to the teacher that lives within me, my own spiritual guide and I will consult that higher presence. I will work with my inner wisdom toward a better me.

I will sit in quiet and listen. I will open my inner ear to hear a deeper voice coming from within me. I will still myself and trust my intuition which is guiding me in the direction that my heart is leaning towards. No one knows me as I know me. I will always consult the teacher who sits within my center.

I seek the counsel of my inner guide.

We only consult the ear because the heart is wanting.

Pascal

▼

The Void

I will enter willingly the state of inner emptiness. I will sit and wait, embrace the silence, welcome the void. The void that I sit in is potentially rich and alive—to avoid it would be to avoid a mystical moment. A visit into a realm beyond. Even the beyond is only a deeper level of the here. The more I can penetrate the illusion that surrounds me, the closer I get to luminescence, to energy, to soul. I will find myself in the oblivion that I fear. I will walk into what feels like nothing and encounter something. I will risk knowing and not knowing.

▼

I embrace the void.

If there were not an utter and absolute dark
Of silence and sheer oblivion
At the core of everything,
How terrible the sun would be,
How ghastly it would be to strike a match,
And make a light.

But the very sun himself is pivoted
Upon the core of pure oblivion.

D. H. Lawrence

Loved Ones

I see value and experience soul evolution in my intimate relationships. Those I love the most help me to see me. They pull on fears and passions, my dreams and desires, and bring them from unconsciousness to consciousness. My love for those I care about motivates me toward a kind of self-honesty that I might otherwise avoid. Because I love them and feel loved by them, I am willing to look at myself. Deep intimacy promotes growth.

I value my loved ones.

Big heart,
wide as a watermelon,
but wise as birth,
there is so much abundance
 in the people I have . . .
and they know me,
they help me unravel,
they listen with ears made of conch shells
they speak back with the wine of the best region.
They are my staff.
They comfort me.

W. B. Yeats

Deus Ex Machina

The ancient Greeks understood our human desire to have a force from above enter our lives, and make sense of the non-sensical. But when I want to find one solution to happiness, I miss the day-to-day experience of living. There is no solution. There is only the process. Wanting an answer puts me at risk of chasing false gods in attempts to locate the soul and find meaning. I will not fall victim to such empty solutions. I will understand that life is meant to be lived, not solved. When I get lost in compulsive thinking and activity, I will take it as a signal that I need to slow down and center myself.

I will not accept quick fixes as a substitute for life.

The world stands out on either side
No wider than the heart is wide
Above the world is stretched the sky
No higher than the soul is high
But east and west will pinch the heart
That cannot keep them pushed apart
And he whose soul is flat
The sky will cave in on him by and by.

Edna St. Vincent Millay

▼

Fully Alive

There is nothing that is not alive with soul energy, and so, hiding from soul is only an illusion. It is like shutting my eyes in a room filled with light and thinking that the light does not exist. Soul is here, now, laced into all that is, was or ever will be.

▼

I let go and float down the
timeless river of soul.

We had the idea that the human was somehow separate from the universe and the scientist would view his or her work as observing the universe from afar. . . . This was actually part of the scientific chemist, the experiences of the human were of a lower order of reality compared to the position of particles. Now we can't hold that dualism any more. . . . From the very beginning, in a sense, the universe was poised to bring forth life, so our existence here can't be seen as something that's alien. And, furthermore, our own deep experiences, the realm of the psyche, the soul, the feelings of the human, this too is as much a part of the universe as the stars are or the gravitational interaction. It is a primary illustration of the underlying order of the universe.

Brian Swimm, *The Soul and the Universe*

▼

My Unconscious as Artist

I will trust my unconscious processes to bring forth my personal truths and solve my inner mysteries. I will carry on a trusting, loving relationship with the parts of myself that I cannot see. If I have faith in my own unconscious process, it will reward me and be my friend. It will act as the artist that reveals to me my own story, my own personal history, my own mythology. My trusting dialogue with my unconscious will allow me to master what in my conscious state seems overwhelming and impossible.

▼

I trust my inner depths.

An individual may . . . struggle with traumatic inner constellations, and, by transformation of the trauma into works of art, achieve a certain mastery over the effect of trauma. . . . the unconscious play work that a subject (person) devotes to any set of received 'issues' incubates an internal organization derived from and devoted to such effort. It could be that an idea will come to mind immediately, but more likely the symphonic idea will derive from intensive unconscious play work.

Christopher Bollas

The All-Soul

I tune in to the soul shared by the universe. I am made of the same soul stuff that the All-Soul is made of; therefore tuning into one is tuning into the other. I have universes of knowledge and wisdom at my fingertips. Like having access to vast computer systems of information from my home, I have access to an all-soul from my own soul. All that is required is sitting and waiting and being willing. I am connected to something greater than myself, part of a universe of wonder. Knowing this gives me an invisible source of strength.

I tune into the All-Soul.

It is an everywhere unity that applies both to soul itself and its various functions. Only the all-soul could have thought or knowledge; to localize thought is to recognize the separate existence of the individual soul.

But . . . the soul is a rational soul, by the very same title by which it is an all-soul, and is called the rational soul, in the sense of being a whole.

Ploinus

Behavior Patterns

When I become aware of destructive behavior patterns, they can serve a wonderful purpose: I can use them as indicators of where my inner work lies. Any situation to which I have a constant over-reaction is telling me something about myself that I need to listen to. My first task is to realize that *the reaction is not fitting the circumstance*, then to sit with that realization, and see through association where it takes me. No one knows my history better than I do, *if I allow myself to know it*.

When I make the decision to come into conscious awareness, to find meaning in my life experience, I begin to experience my life as an adventure—my adventure. When I can raise the source of the unwanted pattern to consciousness to better understand where my pain or reaction stems from, I can begin to see it for what it is and let it go. Then I am no longer repeating history, I am making it.

I co-create my world.

The most terrifying thing is to accept oneself completely.

Carl Jung

▼

Detachment

Practicing detachment is a way to gain perspective on my affairs in life, so that they do not have the power to absorb and run me. Compulsiveness can be seen as an inability to view thought with any level of detachment—a compulsive relationship with my own inner processes. Detachment allows me to be with myself rather than lose myself in every thought that passes through my mind. Practicing detachment helps me to set inner boundaries. When my energy flows willy-nilly into every issue, the energy is no longer under my command but belongs to the thought that has taken it over. Boundaries start from within. Not becoming lost or taken over by my own thoughts is the beginning of setting personal boundaries. I will keep my mind and life clear and centered so that I know from within when I have gone too far.

▼

I am centered from within.

No where can a man find a quieter or more untroubled retreat than in his own soul.

Marcus Aurelius

Meditation in Action

I will allow myself to have a simple relationship with activities, so that they may become a meditation in action. When thoughts arise throughout this process that seem to be demanding my attention, rather than give them attention and energy, I will not further feed them; instead, I will allow them to pass by, simply observing them and letting them go. I will try to get a sense of the transparent quality of thought and action in my life. I live from a deep place within me. I take an action but I am not the action. I have a thought but I am not the thought. I am something deeper and more constant.

I am aligned with an invisible life force.

The joy inherent in simplicity . . . here is not pleasurable in the ordinary sense but is an ultimate and fundamental sense of freedom . . . therefore, the attitude one brings to meditation practice should be very simple, not based upon trying to collect pleasure or avoid pain. Rather, meditation is a natural process, working on the material of pain and pleasure as the path.

Chogyam Trungpha

The Balanced Moment

Today I look for balance in my thinking and my living. Soul is present in the balanced moment. I do not need to look for soul experience in every hot and promising gimmick. Why should I look outside myself for something that exists within me? Why should I continually set myself up for disappointment by giving away my power, by assigning more meaning and life to the promise of a future experience than to the actual experience that I am engaged in right now? Soul is present in me, it is made manifest through me. I will be still and wait for the experience of soul.

I trust soul's presence within me.

Anything carried to an extreme kills itself by being clever and promising magic. In man's effort to understand man, it is foolhardy to look for the complete answer. It does not exist. A new religion comes over the horizon every year and promises salvation to those who would believe. . . . I see change as a point that one strives toward but never gets to.

Thomas F. Fogarty, M.D.

Appreciating the Day

Today I will be aware of the temporary nature of my life. Each day I have is all that I have for certain. If I let today go by unnoticed, unappreciated, unlived, I will not get it back again. It is the little things that make a life. Slowing down, feeling and enjoying where I am and what I have is what will make my day feel good to me. My relationship with soul deepens in the here and now, by sinking into the moment. When I move too quickly, I have no time to process my activities and encounters, no time to smell the roses.

I will relax and enjoy my day.

Without a clear view of death, there is no order, no sobriety, no beauty. Sorcerers struggle to gain this crucial insight in order to help them realize at the deepest possible level that they have no assurance whatsoever their lives will continue beyond the moment. That realization gives sorcerers the courage to be patient and yet take action, courage to be acquiescent without being stupid.

Carlos Castaneda

Perspective

I will laugh at the little absurdities I encounter throughout my day. The fits and misfits in daily routine that ordinarily get me frustrated and annoyed are not worth it. Today I will let them come and go without much attention or unnecessary energy. When I embarrass myself or feel inept, or when other people act foolish for reasons I assume to be less than noble, rather than get angry or judgmental, I will laugh at the silliness of it all. When I feel myself tensing up or notice my responses to be brittle, I will move back an inch within my mind and let my perspective change. I will take a breath and wait a beat. I will keep my sense of humor.

I will play with alternative perspectives.

Who has not heard with relish how children giggle at the absurd things they see, and the falseness of telephone voices they often hear? To turn things around or upside down is the imagination's way of maintaining a perspective on the pro forma irrationalities of social conformity. When we can see even ourselves as funny, it eases this daily living in such close proximity with ourselves.

Joan M. Erickson

Worship

I will worship the divine nature of life. Life and beauty show themselves to me all the time. I see evidence of God every time I turn my head or look within the magnificence of my own soul. All the hours of my day are opportunities to experience soul at work in the world. In fact, this is where I wish to learn to identify soul—in an uncommon/common gesture from someone, in the play of a child, in the kindness of another person. Today I will look for opportunities to notice soul energy in the circumstances that surround me, and I will create opportunities to let the soul within me express itself.

Worship is an everyday thing.

Some keep the Sabbath going to Church—
I keep it, staying at home—
With a Bobolink for a chorister—
And an orchard, for a dome—
. . . so instead of getting to Heaven, at last—
I'm going, all along.

Emily Dickinson

▼

Human Life

I am here, therefore I am. I exist. I am life and love and soul. Any point of view different from this may be seen as a sort of denial, a psychological flight from truth, an emotional defense. I am surrounded by all of life—I come from life, I am life and I will return to life.

▼

I celebrate life.

If there is a God, then God must be always in inter-action with nature. The universe is a cosmic adventure, a God story. God is not only an external carpenter who can create the universe, our God has persuasive, provoc-ative power and is constantly co-creating the universe. The universe is materially built from about 90 elements, all out of one creative source. When we speak of one source for all things, one energy out of which all else has come, we are describing soul. We are also concurring with the story of creation, the story of Genesis, this one soul energy from which all life springs. All of what we are, our physical energy toward movement, feeling, beings, perception have their origins in this singular energy event. All that is comes from one source. The birth of the universe is the energy upon which we live.

David Griffin

Soulmaking and Suffering

Suffering purifies the soul. Working through problems is painful and confusing but allows me to use life circumstances as part of my path toward soul; grist for the mill of soulmaking. Running away from or not fully processing and reintegrating suffering is running away from my full self. Parts of me will be left behind, encased in an unfelt moment of my life, unattended to, frozen and hardened. This frozenness will block the soul until such time when I am willing to thaw out, to relax and let be what will be, to pass through the eye of the needle. There is a truth and an honesty to real suffering that allows me to return to myself, to restore my insides. My willingness to suffer means that I can grow and expand because I am not leaving important aspects of myself untouched and unseen. When I am willing to feel the pain, I inherit the joy.

I need not be a stranger to suffering.

Call the world if you please, the veil of soulmaking.

John Keats

The I-Thou Relationship

When I allow myself to see the world as a thou rather than as an it, it comes to life in the palm of my hands. When the world becomes what Martin Buber calls a thou, it has the same life that I feel I have; there is an exchange of energies that allows me to feel held and nurtured by the presence of life and spirit. When I see the world as an it, I feel lonely and isolated. Everything surrounding me is lifeless and without spirit. When I see the world only as an I-it relationship, I don't allow for the exchange of energy from object to self because I don't recognize that what is around me is as alive as I am. It is my recognition of this soul energy or love energy, my acceptance of the I-thou, that transforms my world. An I-thou relationship allows me to recognize life in all that surrounds me—the same life that I feel to be within me.

All life is equally weighted.

Instead of standing on the shore and proving to ourselves that the ocean cannot carry us, let us venture on its waters—just to see.

Pierre Teilhard de Chardin

▼

Making Room for Grace

Grace can evidence itself in the way I deal with my spouse, my children, those I work with and even my inner thoughts. When I manipulate my feelings to be "better" than they are by taking the high road and supposedly showing someone else up, I am not growing in my relationship with soul. Grace asks me to accept my real feelings as they are, along with the humanity and reality of those of another, and to still be willing to step aside, let go and allow grace to enter a situation.

When I hold on to resentment because I do not want someone who has hurt me to get off the hook, I will recognize that when I keep them on the hook I keep myself at exactly the same place. Setting them free is setting myself free. Retribution is a dynamic, a circle that never ends. It requires high maintenance, and I am the one busy maintaining it.

▼

I re-examine my need for retribution.

A man that studieth revenge keeps his own wounds green, which otherwise would heal and do well.

Francis Bacon

▼

Day-at-a-Time Living

Sometimes I see life as holding only a limited amount of satisfying activities. I feel that if I do not do them all in the same month, gobble them all down in the same year, they will be gone. Living a day at a time sees that I cannot be in two places at once. Setting priorities or doing only the amount of activity that is comfortable has no bearing on what will be available in the future. All that it really means is that by the time the future comes, I will be able to be in it in the same way I am in the present, that I will not have burnt myself out with anxiety, worry and unnecessary stress. All I can really live in is this moment. If I miss it, it will be gone; it will have meant nothing. If I live it, it can give me all the life contained within it and I will have it as a feeling memory to carry within me. I can only be here now—a flight from the moment is a flight from myself.

▼

I live one day at a time.

Every creative act requires elimination and simplification. Simplification results from a realization of what is essential.

Hans Hoffmann

Feeling Fear

My greatest sense of fear is caused by my own unwillingness to feel fear that I carry. Refusing to feel natural inner fear gives it tremendous power over me. Denying my own fear gives it a life of its own. Fear is a basic human feeling, and we all have it. How many of my troubles arise from "refused fear?" Refusing to feel my own fear makes me a prisoner of my projections and anxieties. Accepting and being with the feeling lets the air clear, so that I can see what surrounds me as it is, rather than how I am afraid it is. When I won't feel the fear that I carry within me, I see it as coming at me from all directions. I create people and situations to be afraid of. When I feel it, I can see things as they are and identify my feelings as my own.

I will experience rather than project my fear.

Nothing in life is to be feared. It is only to be understood.

Marie Curie

Agape

Love, particularly *agape*, aligns me with spiritual energy and transforms the world around me into an encounter with soul. More than a sentiment, love is a state of awareness. To enter into a state of love is to be present with soul. Soul and life and love are somehow all together—enter one and you are with the others. Opening my heart to love, even when it is hard to do, moves me to another level of inner experience. I am the immediate benefactor of the love I feel, as I am the first person who feels it. When I am centered through love, the world becomes less threatening. Anything that I can love loses some of its power to hurt and trigger me because love is a transcendent feeling. It puts me in line with the quiet dominion of all things. It allows me to be in tune—to be truly alive.

▼

I choose to experience love.

One cannot be strong without love. For love is not an irrelevant emotion; it is the blood of life, the power of reunion of the separated.

Paul Tillich

Struggle

My search for selfhood is defined not only by how well I am able to acquire new knowledge, but how well I am able to struggle. Selfhood comes with my ability to sit with deeper and deeper levels of what I already "know" but am not fully conscious of, and my willingness to tolerate the intensity of rigorous self-honesty. I need, in a sense, to pass through a smaller self in order to move into a larger self; to take a leap of faith, a free-fall into my own nothingness, my soul, or that within me that is without time, place, circumstance, that within me that is eternal, infinite and somehow connected with a source of energy beyond me. When I can struggle with my own pain, I can sort out the distortions and illusions that keep me from seeing clearly. Like cleaning the dust from a window so that I can see through it, I will clean the dust from my mind so I can see through it to the truth of the soul.

I am willing to struggle.

What one knows is, in youth, of little moment; they know enough who know how to learn.

Henry Adams

Inner Life

I am a container of soul energy; as much as the sun, the leaves and the flowers, I, too, grow and express life. Nature lives within me and I within nature. Soul is inseparable from life and I am a part of life. There is nothing in this universe that is not alive and teeming with neurons. There is no state of non-life, only a state of shutdown. I can choose not to experience life, but life will go on being alive nonetheless. Experiencing it is a subtle shift, a letting in, the opening of an inner door. There is a world within me waiting to be experienced. Today I will allow myself to open to the door and say yes.

I experience a subtle shift within me.

And are those your songs that are echoing in the dark caves of my being? Who but you can hear the hum of the crowded hours that sounds in my veins to-day, the glad steps that dance in my breast, the clamour of the restless life beating its wings in my body?

Rabindranath Tagore

Mind

My mind shapes my life. It is my control room, the place from which I navigate the waters of my world. My thoughts have dynamic power. If radio waves can travel on air waves, then surely my thoughts do, too. What I accept as my reality within my mind exists in living particles and may eventually manifest and evidence itself in my world. My mind is a living part of the universe. It is programmed in, made of the same stuff and designed to operate in this context. The stuff of my mind is the stuff of this living world. What I think is my contribution; it is felt by others, it has impact on my world. I change my life first by changing my thoughts. I contribute positively to society when I carry positive thoughts toward and about it.

I am responsible for what
lives inside my mind.

All that is comes from the mind; it is based on the mind; it is fashioned by the mind.

The Pali Canon

March

Ever since man existed he has sought life's meaning. . . . Life's meaning rests in the eye of the beholder. Life is so immense and complex that there is no one truth. . . . Yet we try to follow our destiny, our passion, our drive. We must live every minute as if it is our first and our last. Never give or receive in return. Never be calculating. Give more than you receive. Let your judgment, above all, be guided by compassion. The meaning of life lies in our desire to help others. Let us show compassion for those weakened by compromise while honoring those who are exceptionally enlightened and humane. Earthly life is an eternal miracle. In a moment of grace, we can grasp eternity in the palm of our hand. This is the gift given to creative individuals who can identify with the mysteries of life through art. It is a divine gift, this spirit of humanity. It is the fight for light over shadow.

Marcel Marceau
from *The Meaning of Life*

▼

The Reality of Thoughts

My thoughts are real. Today, if I wish to see a change in my life I will first envision it in my mind. I will see myself operating in my world as I would like to operate. I will accept my thoughts as powerful and real. I will behave upon the stage within my mind, in the way I wish to behave in the outside world. I will hold the image of how I would like a situation to be, interact with it, smell it, taste it, feel it, be it. Then I will let it go. I will repeat this process over and over again as I go about my day. When I can shape my own thoughts and believe and trust in them, I am choosing how I want to be; I am practicing in my mind. What I can see as possible for myself within my own mind, I can see as possible in my life.

▼

I acknowledge my thoughts as real.

Beholding beauty with the eye of the mind, he will be enabled to bring forth not images of beauty, but realities (for he has hold not of an image but of reality).

Plato

Criticism

I will observe myself in action the next time I find myself being excessively critical of others. Being critical of other people's business comes from comparing myself to them; from a misguided attempt to justify my own position by invalidating theirs. That only overwhelms me and makes me unable to accomplish what suits my own life and feels right to me. When I compare, I tend to compare my aspirations with results accomplished by others; I compare my insides with their outsides.

What I have to offer is unique. All I need for a soul growth experience is the experience of self-expansion. It is being fully engaged in an activity that causes growth for me. It is not in finding the perfect activity, but the perfect relationship with an activity that will allow me to balance my inner and outer worlds, to express myself and to take in what is around me.

I look for the real motivation
beneath criticism.

The mind is its own place, and in itself, can make a Heaven of Hell, a Hell of Heaven.

John Milton

▼

On Being Misled

This world is full of illusion. Status, success, beauty and wealth all provide only limited pleasure. When I make them an ultimate goal, I set myself up for a bitter disappointment. These things carry great glitter and allure. For centuries people have tossed aside real love and true relationship to respond to the distant song of the siren. The beautiful song of the siren in the *Odyssey* caused the sailors to lose their way, to steer into the rocks and eventually to shipwreck. Our modern world has its own version of this song. How many people have ruined perfectly good lives in pursuit of a dream of happiness, only to find that they walked right by happiness and themselves on their way toward an illusion? True happiness comes from a life well lived and love well shared—it issues from the heart.

▼

I will not be fooled by fanciful images.

Beware lest you lose the substance by grasping at the shadow.

Aesop

▼

Simplifying

I will simplify my day today. Each and every task that I need to accomplish can be either broken down and simplified or made more complicated. It is up to me. I will look at the tasks of my day that make me anxious and I will see how to make them less complicated. I will let go of my compulsivity and simply do what needs to be done. I will simplify my mindset. Much of what I experience as complication begins in my mind. It is a subtle hanging on to small circumstances and interactions, or unnecessary anxiety over situations, that only hurts me and creates more anxiety. There is always some way to simplify my thinking, feeling and behavior. This is an important step toward making space in my life for soul to come forward.

▼

I will simplify my day.

Why do you hasten to remove anything which hurts your eye, while if something affects your soul you postpone the cure until next year?

Horace

▼

Out of Hiding

I will bring my soul out of hiding and unlock it from narrow definition. No one has jurisdiction over *my* soul. It belongs to me. Through it I can experience a universe full of wonder and mystery.

▼

I take ownership of my soul.

For me a key moment in the history of reductionism was the year 1600, when the church burned Giordano Bruno, a theologian and a scientist, at the stake. . . . Realizing that these believers can be kind of violent people, they said, "You people take the soul and we'll take the universe and the body." So science went its way and found the basic power of the universe in this century with the spread of the atom, but the result was that science went astray without a conscience, without a sense of justice that you get from religious tradition. And so in this century, science has sold its soul to the military, to petrochemical corporations, etc., etc. Meanwhile the church having surrendered the universe introverted the soul, made it more and more puny and more and more introspective. So the soul became something smaller and smaller, cut off from the universe.

Matthew Fox

Personal Power

I can do a great deal to impact my world for the better without making major lifestyle changes. I recognize that this world will change only when the people in it change. It is people who have the power to destroy or save this planet. Today I resolve to channel my personal power toward good, to open myself to be worked through and with. The world in which I live is my world, it is all that I have. If I see myself as powerless, it will only depotentiate me and make me feel impotent. That is a position I choose not to take today.

▼

I am not a victim.

There are three areas of activity in which we can contribute: in our actions, we can reduce our contribution to destruction through altering our consumption habits, our waste, our choices and our way of working; in our behaviour, we can love ourselves more, and treat others as we would have them treat us; and in our inner life, we can visualise world solutions, work on ourselves to become clearer and more open and phase out negative beliefs—such as the anticipation of catastrophe.

The Only Planet of Choice

▼

Seeing Reality

I treasure my world today. I notice the little
things. I look for magic and beauty and when I see it,
I stay a little longer. I appreciate, I love, I look for
what is alive and beautiful. I feel life and I am aware
of my experience of pleasure. I experience firsthand
the mystery of the universe. I engage to my fullest
capacity in the adventure of living. I need not go to a
museum to see art hung on a wall today because I am
surrounded by art. It is my perception that turns any
single moment into a work of art, that elevates and
celebrates the ordinary. Why should I not be a
philosopher about life or go through my day with the
eye of an artist? Beauty is in the eye of the beholder.

▼

I behold beauty.

*We should feel that it is wonderful to be in this world.
How wonderful it is to see yellow, blue and green, purple
and black! All of these colors are provided for us. We feel
hot and cold; we taste sweet and sour. We have these
sensations and we deserve them. They are good.*

Chögyan Trungpa

The First Move

I will consciously let go of my stubbornness toward life. I will open myself to love. To move toward love is to invite an energy state into being, to manifest soul. All that is necessary to alter my state of awareness is calm, relaxation and a mental attitude that serenely expects love's energy to be present. Once I am in that state, my thinking and feeling will be affected. Resting in the energy of love creates a shift in perception. Much of my life is lived within my mind. When I open myself to feeling love, I will experience my life differently. I will see and feel through the lenses of love. My life may not fundamentally change, but my *experience* of it will. I will give life a fair opportunity to show its beauty to me, rather than insist on it following my script before I give it my seal of approval. I will stop, be still and tune into what life has to say to me.

I will be patient with life.

I do not cut my life up into days but my days into lives, each day, each hour, an entire life.

Juan Ramón Jiménez

The Starry Night

I live in a magical universe. Everywhere I witness the mystery of life that surrounds me. When I close my eyes, mind and heart to this adventure, I inure myself to my own potential for living with soul. In order to live with soul, I need to learn to recognize it in the world that surrounds me. Soul throbs and moves in every living particle. If I experience soul in the small, I am accessing it in the large, and when I experience it in the large, I am accessing it in the small.

I will open to this soul-filled world.

What about the awe you felt when your child was born, when you first made love, or with the starry night? What about the awe astronauts have experienced on the moon? They all came back mystics. Their souls changed up there. You see the opposite of awe is taking it all for granted and our civilization has been taking it for granted for a long time. That's one reason why we're bored and we're violent and we don't have reverence and, therefore, a sense of the sacred toward the soil, the waters and the air.

Matthew Fox

One Particle

I am one with the life that surrounds me. To live in the here and now is to be present to all of life's potentiality. Seeking refuge from the here and now requires my use of defenses in order to shut down experience. Preoccupation, obsessive thinking, escapism, numbing out or acting out—all of these are attempts to move away from the present moment.

The theory of quantum physics verifies the Eastern philosophical view that all life is alive and present in the moment. Billions of tiny neurons intersect and pass through a single given point in the here and now. In other words, each point in the now is a sort of transistor for neuronal movement. It is as if I were bathed in a bath of neurons at all times. Right now life surrounds me, moves through me, carries me on a wave of which I am part and parcel.

I rest in the knowledge that
I am one with all life.

At the still point of the turning world . . . Neither from nor towards; at the still point, there the dance is.

T. S. Eliot

78

Anger

I can see anger as information for me in getting to know my own personality. Anger can be seen as energy, energy that can be used to motivate self-affirming action. For instance, if I am angry that I am being left out of a situation by my employer, strolling into the employer's office and getting mad is only going to exacerbate the problem. The anger can be used to inform me that I am not happy with the situation, and the energy from the anger can propel me into taking an action on my own behalf. The action may have apparently little to do with the anger. It may be doing something, some bit of work unusually well, or bringing to the employer's attention something that I accomplished. In that case, anger is motivating me to take action that will be constructive. The energy from the anger is being used to further my cause, to help to position myself in a way that will feel better to me.

I will use my anger constructively.

He who doesn't know anger doesn't know anything.
He doesn't know the immediate.

Henri Michaux

Accepting the Past

Pain and trauma from my past cannot be changed. They can only be healed. I am lucky to be born at a time when so much help is available. Lucky that I don't have to suffer in silence, lucky that I have resources. Today I will resolve to reach out for the help I need to heal old wounds that block my path toward soul.

▼

I can ask for help.

The first and fundamental challenge for . . . a person is to confront his fate as it is, to reconcile himself to the fact that he did receive a bad deal, to know that justice is irrelevant, that no one will ever make up for the emptiness and the pain of those first . . . years. The past cannot be changed—it can only be acknowledged and learned from. It is one's destiny. It can be absorbed and mitigated by new experiences, but it cannot be changed or erased. He only adds insult to injury by going on the rest of his life knocking his head against the same stone wall. Fortunately, psychotherapy can be a vehicle through which human beings may become more aware of and compensate for such implanted destiny.

Rollo May

Struggle

In order to grow, we must struggle. Children struggle as they move through developmental stages, sorting and resorting what they learn and adapting it to new challenges. Our brain grows with use; new information creates brain growth and alters cell assemblies or particular constellations of memories. Part of struggling is working through previous stages into new ones, changing thoughts and behavior patterns, continually shaping and reshaping the self. When I am able to struggle, I can change, and I can allow others to change in my presence. I can move through stages of life without getting marooned in one because I can't face the anguish of the struggle toward a new one.

I am willing to struggle.

The beauty of the soul shines out when a man bears with composure one heavy mischance after another, not because he does not feel them, but because he is a man of high and heroic temper.

Aristotle

Looking into Life

I will look into rather than at life. I will move toward the experience of love. More than a sentiment, love is an energy. Each living particle has the energy of love and soul encoded into it. Treating love as a sentiment traps it into a thought or a feeling, rather than allowing it to flow freely through the waters of life. Thinking loving thoughts or feeling loving feelings helps to set up the mind or brain to be open to the experience of love. Thoughts and feelings open the door through which love can enter and be present. There are no barriers in the world of love. The barriers we erect are created by the mind. Love is. Love exists as a fundamental energy synonymous with soul. When I look into the world through the eyes of love, that is, when I experience life while in a loving state of mind, I see it differently. My whole perspective changes when I carry love in my mind and heart.

I look through the lenses of love.

It is only with the heart that one can see rightly; what is essential is invisible to the eye.

Antoine de Saint Exupéry

82

Creating Good

If I accept my mind as being truly creative and having genuine power in my life, then the state of my life is dramatically affected by my inner beliefs, by what I have accepted to be truths about myself and my world. What a sobering thought. I, by my thinking and through my attitudes, profoundly influence and shape my life. I want to think that this is New Age psycho-babble, but something in me has already observed this process at work. The changes that I have made for the better began first in my mind—originated as a thought that there might be a better way.

I will take seriously what goes through my mind.

Mind is the creator of everything. You should therefore guide it to create only good. If you cling to a certain thought with dynamic will power, it finally assumes a tangible outward form. When you are able to employ your will always for constructive purposes, you become the controller of your destiny.

Paramahansa Yogananda

The Environment

The environment in which I live is a part of me. The feeling that I have of being able to separate myself from the world I live in is an illusion. I am tied to nature and dependent on it for my survival. I am an animal and share many of the functions of the animal kingdom. It is insanity to think that I can destroy the environment without destroying myself. Nature and I are a part of each other. I follow the patterns of nature, I am physically in tune with the seasons. This world and I are meant to dance together, to live in harmony. It is a strange alienation that keeps me from recognizing my natural place in the scheme of things. It is a form of denial. This world is alive just as I am, we thrive or we perish together.

I am in tune with my natural being.

It is only logical that the pauperization of our soul and the soul of society coincides with the pauperization of the environment. One is the cause and the reflection of the other.

Paolo Soleri

Grace versus Justice

I recognize today that when I carry resentment within me, I am held down and back by the strength of my own feeling. The tree does not know that it elicits in me a feeling of serenity. A sunset may not know that it gives me a feeling of safety and warmth—just as the person I resent likely does not know the extent of the hidden anger that I carry daily in my heart. I am not free when resentment drags on my soul force, dissipating its energy in old grudges.

I cannot break free alone. All the wisdom in the world cannot put back in my heart the love yearned for but never received, or had but lost. Whatever the wound, it may take more than I have to heal it. I need to ask and pray for grace to enter my life and help me do what feels impossible. I will pray for grace to move me toward freedom and away from my wish to destroy, knowing that I cannot destroy another without wounding myself.

I pray for grace.

To forgive is the best revenge.

The Bible

▼

Character

I will remember today that there is no substitute for character. Building a good and wholesome character is the work of a lifetime, and the fuel behind it is faith and a basic sense of decency. Who I am is at the center of all that I do and is what I bring to each moment of my life that is wholly my own, wholly unique. Each day, starting today, I build who I am.

▼

My character is built from within.

It is character that communicates most eloquently. As Emerson once put it, "What you are shouts so loudly in my ears I cannot hear what you say." There are, of course, situations where people have character strength but they lack communication skills, and that undoubtedly affects the quality of relationships as well. But the effects are still secondary.

In the last analysis, what we are communicates far more eloquently than anything we say or do. We all know it. There are people we trust absolutely because we know their character. Whether they're eloquent or not, whether they have the human relations techniques or not, we trust them, and we work successfully with them.

Stephen R. Covey

Art and Soul

Art can light a path toward soul. It can create a moment of connection to something beyond the moment. Art can awaken in me quick joy when time disappears, when I become the experiencer and the experienced—when my mind ceases to question and search and rests only in the moment. Art blazes a pathway toward soul. I will use art and let it take me with it to a transcendent state. I will listen to its language of metaphor. Soul is a quiet thing, waiting to be slowly born into the here and now. Art is a vehicle that leads me toward soul.

I recognize the soul experience.

For the moment nothing but an ineffable joy and exaltation remained. It is impossible fully to describe the experience. It was like the effect of some great orchestra, when all the separate notes have melted into one swelling harmony, that leaves the listener conscious of nothing save that his soul is being wafted upwards and almost bursting with its own emotion.

William James

▼

Wisdom and Perception

Taking the time to perceive a circumstance helps me to be less superficial and understand complicated undercurrents more clearly. Once I am able to perceive more fully all the dynamics present, I will use wisdom to inform my actions. Oftentimes non-action is the wisest course to take. If I am capable of non-action, my actions will have more meaning and stronger effect. Perception and wisdom allow me to live a more satisfying inner life; they let me enjoy the world around me without getting embroiled and entangled in it. Enmeshment only drains my energy and ties up my inner resources. Mindful detachment can actually allow me to participate more fully in life.

▼

I will practice cultivating wisdom and
perception in one affair today.

Acquire Wisdom, acquire Perception.
Never forget her, never deviate from my words.
Do not desert her, she will keep you safe.
Love her, she will watch over you.

Prov. 4:5-8

▼

Parent/Child Relationship

When I talk about having a mature relationship with my parents, it is really a process of seeing them as human. My parents' opinion was only theirs; there is another world out there—I may see the whole situation differently. They are not the people who define me.

Painful feelings toward my parents are natural. When I learn that my parents do not die from my anger and that I do not lose the love relationship with my parents because of negative feelings, then being dependent in intimate relationships later in life becomes less threatening. If the love and hate are not understood and accommodated within this deep parent/child relationship, later intimate relationships that arouse feelings of dependency will seem frightening.

Anger toward the parent is as natural as love toward the parent, and this is true of any deep relationship.

▼

I can live with both the love and hate that are part of deep dependent relationships.

Let my heart be wise. It is the god's best gift.

Euripides

An Individual

I am an individual able to stand on my own, while still maintaining genuine connection with others. I am not an island unto myself, nor am I a nondistinct part of the mass. I see my life as a process of getting to know myself, of exploring the contents of my mind and heart, which will in turn allow me to understand myself and others. I have a right to self-define.

I enjoy being me.

Only the man who can consciously assent to the power of the inner voice becomes a personality and only a personality can find a proper place in the collectivity; only personalities have the power to create a community, that is, to become integral parts of a human group and not merely a number in the mass. For the mass is only a sum of individuals and can never, like a community, become a living organism that receives and bestows life. Thus, self realization, both in the individual and in the extra personal, collective sense, becomes a moral decision, and it is this moral decision which leads us to the process of self fulfillment called individuation. . . . it also implies becoming one's own self.

Carl Jung

Soul in Adversity

I will use the most painful situations in my life as a catalyst for soul growth. In deep trials lie opportunities to come closer to the core of myself and to draw out, from my inner depths, strength and spirituality that I didn't know were there. As I would stand near to a loving parent when I felt insecure as a child, so I will stand nearer to God when trouble comes.

Adversity is an opportunity
for soul growth.

When my husband, Benigno, was imprisoned at the start of martial law in 1972, we thought life was over. We could not understand this injustice. But I asked myself what sins Jesus had committed to make His sacrifice justified, and I realized we are all faced with injustices. If we have faith, we can overcome every difficulty. My husband had not been a religious person, but once he was in jail, God was the only one he could turn to. Through reading the Bible and putting his destiny in God's hands, he become strongest at the time he felt weakest.

Corazon Aquino

A Song in My Heart

I will carry a song within my heart today. I will feel the rhythm of my soul's energy pulsing through me. No one but me has access to my soul. If I do not invite it into expression then it will not, cannot come; I am the vehicle through which it finds expression. I am the carrier of spirit. I will allow soul to surface in my heart, mind and point of view.

A spirit finds its highest and finest life through the human hand. My recognition of God in man allows God to come forward in my community to work through people. What I do today I will do soulfully, whether it be taking a walk, eating breakfast or visiting with a friend. Soul is everywhere, always present. Today I will be with and invite the presence of soul.

▼

I will listen and hear music.

The last of the light of the sun
That had died in the west
Still lived for one song more
In a thrush's bleats.

Robert Frost

▼

Wounds

I will release myself from the compulsion to repeat destructive and painful patterns, by being willing to acknowledge the wounds that lie beneath them. In my attempts to keep these wounds from being known, I keep myself away from important parts of myself. Then I seek out situations that will allow my wounds to surface and be felt. My unconscious knows what it is carrying within it and wants it to come to the surface so that it can heal. While I hold it in darkness, I keep an emotional infection from getting the light and air that it needs to heal. I will not glorify living mindlessly and without pain. I will use my pain to cleanse my self.

▼

I am willing to acknowledge my wounds.

I am ill because of wounds to the soul, to the deep emotional self, and the wounds to the soul take a long, long time, only time can help and patience, and a certain difficult repentance, long difficult repentance, realization of life's mistakes and the freeing of one's self from the endless repetition of the mistake . . . has chosen to sanctify.

D. H. Lawrence

▼

Tears

True grief will cleanse my soul. I will trust it and allow it to do its healing work. Nature has built a mechanism into me for releasing emotional pain—I know that experiencing my feelings is the surest and quickest way in and out of the pain. I will not be at war with my own insides, asking them to hide from me, creating an inner person that I don't want anyone to see. The person that I pretend to hide from the world, I am really hiding from me. Today I know that there is no need for that—what I keep in hiding only grows in strength, what I let go of will set me free. When I cry, I release enzymes from my body. It is a chemical release, nature's way of letting pain leave me. I will not deny myself the benefit of this inner physician.

▼

Tears cleanse my soul.

Where praise already is the only place grief ought to go,
that water spirit of the pools of tears; she watches over
our defeats to make sure the water rises clear from the
same rock.

Rainer Maria Rilke

Miracles

Today I will see miracles in ordinary living. I will train my eye and my inner vision to notice the wondrous and mystical world that surrounds me. Why do I need proof of eternity and the essential creative power of the universe—can't I perceive it by holding, in my hand, just one flower; or by watching the sun disappear behind the horizon, or rising to the song of birds? Living itself is a miracle. When I learn to see the miraculous that is a part of the world I live in, I will find it easier to allow soul to be alive within me. Nothing less than this would be in tune with this alive universe in which I live.

I will see miracles in ordinary life.

Why, who makes much of a miracle?
As to me, I know of nothing else but miracles,
Whether I walk the streets of Manhattan,
Or dart my sight over the roofs of houses toward the sky. . . .
Every cubic inch of space is a miracle,
Every square yard of the surface of the earth
Is spread with the same.

Walt Whitman

Transcending the Flesh

I will not use the shortcomings in this world as an excuse for the shortcomings in me. My path is not to imitate what is wrong, but to lead in what is right. Each positive example I set by actually embodying or being what I believe in improves this world.

I am willing to lead.

I was doing a show on victims confronting their criminals. A 17-year-old girl was on the air speaking to the man who, four years earlier, had beaten her beyond recognition and left her for dead. She'd had 17 surgeries and complete facial reconstruction. She said to him, "I don't hate you. I hate what you did to me. And I have had to learn to forgive you so I could go on with my own life." To this day it is the most powerful thing I've ever seen. In that moment, she expressed why we're here—to learn to love in spite of the human condition, to transcend the human condition of being fearful. We get so bogged down in worldly things we don't understand that we're here for a spiritual quest. Understanding that this is a journey is the most exciting part of being human. It has revolutionized my life.

Oprah Winfrey

Asking for Help

I can accomplish a lot in life if I am willing to ask for help. The psychological and emotional position of asking for help humbles and opens me up to new learning; it automatically lowers my defenses.

On a spiritual level, the words "seek and you shall find, knock and the door shall be opened unto you" describe an inner reaching toward something beyond the temporal experience, an acknowledgment of forces beyond the illusion of reality. Asking for help on this level connects me with the quantum physical level or the mind of God; it allows spirit to work in my life. There are forces beyond my vision that are alive and operational. Asking for help invites them to work in my life. It moves me from my stuck position so that I can open up to change. It promotes a shift in my awareness.

I can and will ask for help.

Faith—is the pierless bridge supporting what we see
Unto the scene that we do not.

Emily Dickinson

Play And Soul

Soul comes in many forms—an eight-year-old child inviting another friend to swing, a raucous game of Red Rover (where you hear your name called out and feel as if you have been chosen by the heavens), in the soft easy pattern of the rope on the blacktop as you jump up and down to "keep the kettle boiling." Children enter a sort of soul state when they play. Time disappears, expands, contracts and loses its relevance and dominion over daily living. Play allows them to enter the here-and-now. They go deeply into themselves, each other and the moment; both the energy that surrounds them and that they manufacture has an electricity and a luminescence to it that is tangible. I will observe the true teachers of play today, to see what lessons I can learn.

I will watch children play.

Did you know, throughout the cosmos they found intelligent life forms that play to play? We are the only ones that play to win. Explains why we have more than our share of losers.

Lily Tomlin

▼

Shedding Light On Darkness

I accept the challenge of soul growth. I have not chosen an easy path—a commitment to see the light also requires a commitment to see the dark. Allowing light and spirit to work in my life is an act of courage and surrender. When the light goes on, it illuminates the entire scene. There is nothing that darkness avoids more than light: wickedness works in the shadows, manipulation depends on no one bringing it out into the open. Once it is out in the light, it cannot maintain the enormous power it exerted in the gray spaces.

I can tolerate light.

When each day / is sacred,
when each hour / is sacred,
when each instant / is sacred,
earth and you / space and you
bearing the sacred / through time
you'll reach / the fields of light

Compline

April

"Yes," I said to the prince. "The house, the stars, the desert—what gives them their beauty is something that is invisible!"

"I am glad," he said, "that you agree with my fox."

As the little prince dropped off to sleep, I took him in my arms and set out walking once more. I felt deeply moved, and stirred. It seemed to me that I was carrying a very fragile treasure. It seemed to me, even, that there was nothing more fragile on all the Earth. In the moonlight I looked at his pale forehead, his closed eyes, his locks of hair that trembled in the wind, and I said to myself: "What I see here is nothing but a shell. What is most important is invisible. . . ."

As his lips opened slightly with the suspicion of a half-smile, I said to myself, again: "What moves me so deeply, about this little prince who is sleeping here, is his loyalty to a flower—the image of a rose that shines through his whole being like the flame of a lamp, even when he is asleep. . . ." And I felt him to be more fragile still. I felt the need of protecting him, as if he himself were a flame that might be extinguished by a little puff of wind. . . .

And, as I walked on so, I found the well, at daybreak.

Antoine de Saint Exupéry
The Little Prince

Being Part of the Magic

I have the power to create, to bring forth, to manifest. My very presence measurably alters my environment. If merely by observing and being I affect what surrounds me, think how much more my thoughts, speech and actions are felt by others. Today, if I feel that I am disappearing, as if I am insignificant or ineffectual, I will remember that this is not possible. I am designed by a higher intelligence to be powerful and to interact in real and meaningful ways. My presence has impact.

I own my effect on my world.

Directly stated, the evolution of the entire universe—stars, elements, life, man—is a process of drawing something out of nothing, out of the utter void of nonbeing. The creative element in the mind of man—that latency which can conceive gods, carve statues, move the heart with the symbols of great poetry, or devise the formulas of modern physics—emerges in as mysterious a fashion as those elementary particles which leap into momentary existence in great cyclotrons, only to vanish again like infinitesimal ghosts.

Lorin Eisley

Guilt

I will take a good look today at the way that I carry guilt and shame. Some guilt is my unconscious telling me where I am not living up to my own standards. But gnawing, painful, irrational guilt is self-destructive. Guilt can help me to know where I have gone off my track, but if it is eating me up inside, it is self-destructive. That kind of guilt keeps me locked in a cycle of wrongdoing. It becomes too painful to feel guilty, so I get rid of the feeling by acting in destructive ways.

Acting the feelings out keeps me from feeling them. They are no longer useful to me as a source of personal information and don't tell me where my inner work lies. When I pile on too much guilt, all I want is to get rid of the feeling. Where did I learn to beat up on myself in this way, and why am I continuing to do it today? It is up to me to be decent and gracious with my own insides. Once I have learned what I need to learn from guilt, I have a right to release it.

▼

I let go of self-destructive guilt.

Self-reflection is the school of wisdom.

Baltasar Gracian

Daily Rituals

Our lack of meaningful ritual causes us to reach for objects outside ourselves for a sense of grounding. If we remain outwardly focused with our meaning existing outside of us, we may experience a spiritual crisis.

One of the ways to reconnect with my self is through rituals in my daily life. Rituals give me a sense of connection to something within me, and through that connection to a transcendent self, something larger than and beyond the everyday me. My rituals can be highly individualized. They may be daily quiet time or meditation, journaling or nature walks. It is important that I identify, cultivate and maintain both private and communal rituals. The important point is the necessity of having regular, ritualized experiences built into my day-to-day living that help my smaller self connect with a larger, or transcendent, self. Personal rituals act as passageways from the temporal to the spiritual world.

▼

I cultivate daily rituals.

The more peculiarly his own a man's character is, the better it fits him.

Cicero

The Politics of Soul Awareness

It would seem that the world is realigning itself to make world war obsolete, and in so doing, it paves the way for me to reduce my own personal wars. To look within, to self-examine, to make inner peace and peace within my personal relationships a true life goal, is to devote myself with sincerity to making the world I live in safe for my children and grandchildren. Soul awareness is the simplest and most effective way to change society. If I really care about the future of this world, I will take care of personal business. First, I will accept and love myself; then I will give this acceptance and love to those close to me. I will take care of my corner of the world. I will make peace at home.

I will do my part.

Peace does not spring full grown, it requires cultivation, it requires patience and care. . . . peace is more than an agreement on paper, it is activity, it is devotion.

President Bill Clinton

▼

Soul Loss

I will respect and protect quiet in my day. Without quiet, my soul cannot rise to the surface of my consciousness. Excessive and pointless busyness keeps me from being with soul. Then I feel a loss of connection with self, and I try to solve it by attaching myself to one more outer experience in an attempt not to feel alone and lost. Again I create disappointment.

▼

The soul that I lost is within me.

There also exists a sleeping sickness of the soul. Its most dangerous aspect is that one is unaware of its coming. That is why you have to be careful. . . . You should realize that your soul suffers if you live superficially. People need times in which to concentrate, when they can search their inmost selves. It is tragic that most men have not achieved this feeling of self-awareness. And finally, when they hear the inner voice they do not want to listen anymore. They carry on as before so as not to be constantly reminded of what they have lost. But as for you, resolve to keep a quiet time. . . . Then your souls can speak to you without being drowned out by the hustle and bustle of everyday life.

Albert Schweitzer

Refused Fear

Psychologists say that many of their patients' troubles arise from "refused fear." It was Franklin Delano Roosevelt who said, "The only thing we have to fear is fear itself." When we allow ourselves to feel fear, fundamental fear that is natural to all of us, we no longer have to devise a thousand ways to run from it. We experience a kind of freedom and learn that fear was only a wall to pass through on the way to self. If we take it seriously by refusing to acknowledge its presence, we give it power. On the other hand, if we accept its presence, sit with it and make it, in a sense, our friend, it loses its solidity and its intense grip; then we are able to move through it and into ourselves.

I feel rather than refuse fear.

Zen comes itself. One must discover the life principle, the mind. The process of finding it (Zen) involves what Jung calls the withdrawal of projections. There must be no running away from life, still less from Zen. Yet we attempt to escape in many ways.

Y. C. Kim

The Quantum Vacuum

I am part of an "unbroken wholeness." The excitement and the mystery of the quantum vacuum, of essential aliveness, is pulsing throughout and around me at all times. I am one with soul. When I feel at loose ends, exhausted, out of touch with myself, I will remind myself that all I need to do is to quiet down, to be still. I do not even need to enter into a state—only to be calm enough so that I can tune into what already is, to allow a state to enter into me. Life lives within me and I live within life. All the forms and permutations of this aliveness are here, happening, evolving and transforming. I am part of a living mystery.

I am one with the natural transformation
of living material.

The quantum vacuum is the underlying reality of all that is and everything that exists including ourselves, this chair, this glass. . . . It's as though there is a God, a sort of unrealized, unbroken wholeness . . . which is trying to realize itself through these excitations, through these disturbances of its own equanimity.

Danah Zohar

▾

Somebody vs. Nobody

Often I interpret a person's somebody-ness through material eyes. If they possess objects and qualities that society values, I consider them somebody. But if I ask these somebodies how they feel deep in their hearts, they might admit that being somebody in the eyes of the world does not keep them from feeling like nobody within themselves. The feeling of being somebody, of connecting to something greater than the self, cannot come from an object or an outside identity. It comes from within, from a connection with soul and life.

This is what soul awareness gives me: that sense of being connected to life in a fundamental way. It allows me to take joy and an attitude of celebration for the simple gift of life, the act of living itself. When I feel connected to something that transcends day-to-day awareness, the vicissitudes of life do not seem greater than my sense of beauty and aliveness, my feeling that life is, after all, worth living.

I am somebody.

A miracle is a shift in perception.

The Course in Miracles

Value

If I have had a true transformation, a genuine awareness of soul integrated into me, then life will be changed both fundamentally and in a thousand ordinary ways.

This shift in perception will do more to alter my society, to alter my world, than any other single act because when people feel good about themselves, they value themselves, others and the world in which they live. Hatred so often arises from a negative feeling about the self. Then, when it is too painful to hate ourselves in isolation, we turn the hatred outward onto everything and anything that we see. When an inner transformation takes place, when we come to see ourselves and our lives as valuable, that is the feeling that gets turned toward the world. When love is turned out toward the world, society changes.

I am a political force, a loving
member of society.

What we must decide is perhaps how we are valuable, rather than how valuable we are.

Edgar Z. Friedenberg

Repression

When I was a child, I sometimes felt overwhelmed by situations that I felt were out of control and so, as a childhood defense, I may have repressed the feelings, such as fear, anger or hurt, associated with particular experiences because I felt I could not cope with them in any other way. When, as an adult, feelings from the past get triggered by a present-day circumstance, I can be confused by my own reaction. I can have a hard time feeling these emtoions as an adult because in addition to triggering the repressed feeling, the fear and terror from childhood associated with the feeling also get triggered. Then, I scare myself all over again. This is one way in which my past can negatively impact my present. Today I will pay attention to what is being triggered within me that may have been repressed at an earlier time in my life.

I will examine repressed material.

A poorly extingusihed fire is quickly re-ignited.

Corneille Setorius

▼

A Breath of Living Spirit

I appreciate the miracle of life. Today I do not need answers and explanations about life in order to feel life is worthwhile. Instead, I will *experience* it. Talking about life is different from experiencing it. Even understanding life is unnecessary if I am really willing to lift the veil that separates me from the mystery of the present moment, and to allow meaning to reveal itself to me. I am willing to have a personal experience of soul. No one need tell me what soul is, no one need give me permission to live in soul awareness. I am here, I am surrounded by inexplicable miracles. It is enough.

I am part of the mystery.

The soul is a breath of living spirit,
That with excellent sensitivity,
permeates the entire body to give it life.
Just so,
The breath of the air makes the earth fruitful.
Thus the air is the soul of the earth,
moistening it: greening it.

Hildegard of Bingen

▼

Unnecessary Expectations

Oftentimes, it is my high expectations of what people can give me or what experiences can bring me that lead me toward disappointment. When I expect something to give me more than it can, I set myself up for feeling gypped.

Expectation sets up a barrier between myself and experience. It makes me feel that if I do not get what I expect to receive, I should block out taking in whatever else may be there for me. My very expectation keeps me from being receptive to what a situation has to give me because I have pre-decided how something must look in order to qualify as a something. Today I will get out of the way of my own expectations.

▼

I am open to what is really happening.

It seems to be the fate of man to seek all his consolations in futurity. The time present is seldom able to fill desire or imagination with immediate enjoyment, and we are forced to supply its deficiencies by recollection or anticipation.

Samuel Johnson

▼

Soul Is Within Me

I am a living expression of the divine energy, a piece of God. This is how God meant it to be, how spirit works through flesh, how the world is an expression of the divine.

▼

I will look within for soul.

Long ago all men were divine, but mankind so abused the privilege that Brahma, the god of all gods, decided the godhead should be taken away from them. But he had to hide it where man would never find it again. "Let us bury it deep in the earth," suggested one god. Brahma said, "No, man will dig down until he finds it." "Then let us throw it into the deepest part of the biggest ocean," proposed another god. "Man will learn to dive and someday come across it," insisted Brahma. "Then it can be hidden in the clouds atop the highest mountain of the Himalayas." "Man will manage to climb that high some day," Brahma pointed out. "I have a better idea. Let us hide it where he will never think to look: inside man himself."

Hindu legend

▼

Suppression

When I start to avoid thoughts that hurt, see it as a strength to "keep a stiff upper lip," I may be using a defense that creates tension within my personality. Tension builds into stress, and stress seeks relief. If too much is suppressed in this manner, it may be released inappropriately, or I may be inclined to reach for a substance or an activity to relieve the stress.

I will try another way today. I will try not to become so identified with a thought that it has to be dealt with harshly. If a thought arouses anxiety within me, it is probably more useful in the long run just to feel it in the moment and allow it to expend its energy. I will observe my thoughts rather than get lost in them. If I do not interfere with them by trying to get rid of them or manipulate them, chances are this entire process will not take more than a few minutes.

▼

I allow myself to feel my anxiety.

Every person's emotions have a front door and a side door by which they may be entered.

Oliver Wendell Holmes

Facing Life

I am willing to pay the price of personal growth. Growth is messy. It is embarrassing at times to struggle for more wholeness, more of me, particularly when other people see it as excessive or infantile. But for me, this is my road to maturity and of meeting life on more honest terms. I know that I have not chosen an easy path in seeking soul enlightenment, but I have heard and stepped to the beat of a different drummer and I want to learn more.

▼

I will do what it takes to be whole.

It costs so much to be a full human being that there are very few who have the enlightenment, or the courage, to pay the price. . . . One has to abandon altogether the search for security, and reach out to the risk of living with both arms. One has to embrace the world like a lover, and not demand an easy return of love. One has to accept pain as a condition of existence. One has to court doubt and darkness as the cost of knowing. One needs a will stubborn in conflict, but apt always to the total acceptance of every consequence of living and dying.

Morris L. West

Tolerating the Pain of Emptiness

I will tolerate the pain of emptiness when it enters my soul or my life. When I am not willing to do this, I cannot get to the other side of the river, to a true soul experience. Instead, I have more children, make more money, take on more work, all in a vain attempt to fill a void that cannot be filled. That hole within me that I fear falling into has to be felt, not filled. This is my own, private spiritual struggle; my own inner battle. No one thing can solve my life or make it so that I will never feel empty inside. Really feeling empty is the first step toward spiritual fullness. It is a dangerous society that tells us that it is wrong to feel empty, that it is a sign of failure. Having the inner resources and strength to actually feel emptiness are what give me the information that I need to organize my life, that tells me what the correct balance between activity and downtime is for me. My emptiness is my teacher and my friend.

I can tolerate my own emptiness.

Seeing is believing, but feeling's the truth.

Thomas Fuller

▼

The Action of Soul

Now is my time for action. Living with soul is a choice I make that benefits me, my family, my country and my world. I contribute to the society in which I live by living as a conscious individual. Soul is political. It is an idea whose time has come, a force that can and will save this world if taken seriously. The soul is as old as forever, re-creating it in the here-and-now is new. I will make soul appropriate to my life and my world today. I will recognize not only its personal impact and meaning, but also its power to transform the world in which I live.

▼

Living consciously is my
contribution to society.

What counts now is not just what we are against, but what we are for. Who leads us is less important than what leads us—what conviction, what courage, what faith—win or lose. A man doesn't save a century, or a civilization, but a militant party wedded to a principle can.

Adlai Stevenson

Self-Caring

I believe in the power of my own experience. I trust my own eyes, my own senses. There is no need for me to be dragged from doctrine to doctrine, from belief to belief. I have an inner voice. When I allow myself to be still and listen, I can hear it. There is a difference between being self-indulgent and self-caring. Self indulgence is an attempt to bribe myself, to get away from what is really going on. Self-caring is treating myself as I wish to be treated. When I am caring rather than indulgent, the messages I get from within are clearer and better reflect truth.

I make up my own mind.

Believe nothing, O monks, merely because you have been told it . . . or because it is traditional, or because you yourselves have imagined it. Do not believe what your teacher tells you merely out of respect for the teacher. But whatsoever, after due examination and analysis, you find to be conducive to the good, the benefit, the welfare of all beings—that do believe and cling to, and take it as your guide.

attributed to Buddha

▼

The Dynamic of Blame

Blaming another person can become a way of positioning the self as a victim. When children are young and see their parents as the entire world, they are extremely vulnerable and dependent upon their parents' opinions. If their parent belittles them and makes them feel in the wrong, they will eventually come to do the same, turning that opinion inward onto themselves. In this case, part of the process of healing will be to turn self-hatred outward—back toward the parent as a way of righting the original distortion. This, however, is only a part of the process. Continued healing will happen when the parent is knocked off the pedestal and no longer seen as the ultimate authority when the parents become human for the child, who is now an adult, and when that child can see them with understanding and perspective, realizing that they, too, had a history.

▼

I am not my parents' opinion of me.

One must first learn to live with one's self before one blames others.

Feodor Dostoyevsky

◆

Abundance

I will ask for abundance. I am constantly limiting myself, clipping around the edges, asking for less because I am afraid of disappointment. I feel guilty at the thought of having abundance and enjoyment. It makes me feel selfish to want. But soul is abundant. Living with the infinite wealth of soul energy, asking spirit to work in my day, is inviting richness and plenty into my life. Perhaps this is a different kind of selfishness—one that connects me with a higher purpose and a greater good, that brings with it a deeper, truer satisfaction with life.

I will ask for more.

I bargained with Life for a penny, / And Life would pay no more, / However I begged at evening / When I counted my scanty store; / For Life is a just employer, / He gives you what you ask, / But once you have set the wages, / Why, you must bear the task. / I worked for a menial's hire, / Only to learn, dismayed, / That any wage I had asked of Life, / Life would have paid.

Jessie B. Rittenhouse

▾

Faith in My World

I am part of an exciting period in history. Those who have given up on the world are not seeing what I am seeing. I see spirit at work. I see deep world cleansing. I see people who are more aware and willing to look at themselves and society. The barricades that used to divide countries and people are falling along with rigid and repressive methods of controlling people. This is a world in flux, moving toward something better.

▾

I will have faith in my world.

This spiritual urge is undeniable. From the beginning of human history, we have been embarked on a search for transcendent meaning. It is as if we were genetically coded to believe that there is a greater force and mystery framing our lives. Which is why the next great improvement in the human condition will occur not through a millennial faith in technology but by uncovering a new, more spiritually satisfying notion of "progress," one that requires a vertical leap of faith, a leap in our inner development. The answer is not to ignore these issues in schools and institutions. It is to fling open the doors.

Norman Lear

▼

Living in Today

I can do well with this day. Though I can take appropriate precautions and make sound plans, whatever problems are present in future days will have to be faced and dealt with then. The future looks scary when I compare it with today. Either I want it to hold the promise of something better or I want a guarantee that it will be as good as today. This fear of my future is really fear of the unknown. An existential terror of waking up one day and finding myself to be an alien in my own life, a stranger in my own skin. Soul is only accessible through the here and now. I can only solve my life for today. I can only live one day at a time.

▼

I will live this day as well as I can.

Anyone can carry his burden, however hard, until nightfall. Anyone can do his work, however hard, for one day. Anyone can live sweetly, patiently, lovingly, purely, till the sun goes down. And this is all that life really means.

Robert Louis Stevenson

Suffering

I recognize that through deep personal suffering comes soul growth. I connect with soul through my inner self. The more deeply I am able to go within, the deeper my relationship with my own soul. Why should life be easy? Isn't my insistence on its being easy a sort of immaturity? Anyone who has truly felt life knows that there is pain along with pleasure, loss along with gain, fullness along with emptiness. There is a purity and a nobility to suffering that brings me closer to my own divine nature and burns away the debris that blocks my path toward soul. My character is formed in the furnace of my soul, shaped from and strengthened constantly by trying to pull out of myself the best that I have to offer at that time. When I turn my back on what is difficult and painful in life, I weaken my character.

I am willing to feel.

When a man's knowledge is sufficient to attain, and his virtue is not sufficient to enable him to hold, whatever he may have gained, he will lose again.

Confucius

Being Earthbound

I will be earthbound today. I will recognize that a higher intelligence has designed this world to be organic. I am, by nature, entirely interdependent. In order to participate in sustaining life. I am organic. I eat, sleep, make love to reproduce and sustain life through my own body. Running from these activities, trying to be above them, is running from my very self.

All that is divine is programmed into all that is alive. The secret of soul lies within this living world. Interdependence is natural and built into the system, and I am part of this system. The trick is to depend to a natural extent, to recognize my human needs and allow them. It is when I try to deny neediness that my needs control me. Then I have to set about meeting them surreptitiously. When I treat them as natural and meet them openly, they do not run me in silence. Truly spiritual people have an earthbound feeling to them: they know they belong here.

I am meant to be here.

The way to do is to be.

Tao Te Ching

▼

A Quiet Love of Life

I love my life today. Waking up, enjoying my morning rituals, easing into my day—all of these little moments provide a pleasant and comfortable entry into morning. Today it is enough just to be alive, just to be here. The richest part of my life is spent in my own mind. The contents of my thoughts and the feeling states they evoke are precious to me, they hold me in an inner world of pleasure and beauty. My soul is with me today. It is here with my morning coffee, the paper, the sunlight streaming through the window, a scattered pile of papers. My soul is not far away and separate—it is the very energy that fuels my thoughts, that moves my hand.

▼

Soul is a daily thing.

Lord, my mind is not noisy with desires,
and my heart has satisfied its longing.
I do not care about religion or anything that is not you.
I have soothed and quieted my soul, like a child at its mother's
*   breast.*
My soul is as peaceful as a child sleeping in its mother's arms.

Psalm 131

▼

Being With Self

I will not chase self today. Rather, I will trust. I will wait for the self to emerge. I will be aware of self. When I try to find self, grab it and hold onto it, I reduce it to what it is not. Self is present in all things and I am present in self. Life is constantly in motion and self moves with the waves of life—of the living particle patterned into all things. When I try to locate self in a particular place, I cannot find it because self is equally present in all things. I cannot hold self. Other people cannot hold or withhold my self. The self I seek is a state that I access through me. I cannot make the experience stationary so that I know where to look to find it. I can only be present within the fluid state of self. Self breathes as I breathe, self is with me and I am within self. We are one.

▼

I will be in the presence of self.

What the superior man seeks is in himself.
What the mean man seeks is in others.

Confucius

▼

Coincidence

I will pay attention to coincidence, knowing that it is at the moment of connection between the inner and outer worlds that my soul and physical world come together. My inner and outer dimensions intersect at these points. They appear accidental, but they are the stitching together of two fabrics, two worlds. It is said that coincidence is God losing anonymity for a moment. I will look at what appear to be meaningless coincidences as God talking to me and guiding me along my path.

▼
I see through coincidence.

By soul wisdom I mean the development of a capacity for self-knowledge in conjunction with an objective sense of the inner qualities of the outer world. The capacity for this conjunction leads to a new image of consciousness that "sees through" events, both inner and outer, finding a circulation going on between them in which a constant re-creation of both the human being and the world takes place. This circulating force or power I shall call soul. The magical world, the inner world, the psychic world is this world of the physical planet and none other.

Robert Sardello

Being an Artist

I will be an artist today and speak what is my innermost truth, share what is in my mind and heart. An artist's job is both to reflect and lead. It is only when I am willing to be honest that I am close to my own art. Art is not about being right. If it were, I would never create. I will decode life in my own way today and express myself as me.

I will be me.

Nobody really knows, why we're here, obviously. There are big pieces missing from the pictures offered us by science and religion. Based on our present knowledge, the whole thing simply doesn't make sense. But what's so wonderful is that we want it to make sense, and our need for meaning drives us relentlessly to create. Cave paintings, totem poles, villages, cathedrals—it is a never-ending process. Sometimes I think we have become the creative gods and goddesses of our myths and dreams. If we do have a purpose, maybe it is to join with the evolutionary process through our complex artistic creation. Our stories and poems and lasers are as significant as diamonds or gold or angelfish.

Anne Rice

Seeing Soul

I stand in awe of the beauty and mystery that surround me. This world need not be more than it is to convince me of the gift of life. I appreciate my life today. If I don't appreciate it now, then that now will turn into hours, the hours to days, the days to months and the months to years, and I will have missed them. The moment is all that I have, what I do not say now will go unsaid, what I do not do now will go undone. What I do not see now, while it surrounds me, will go unseen. Everywhere my eye turns there is more of life. The life of spirit is at my fingertips, painted into each landscape, sewn into each seed, blossoming into each and every tree and flower and blade of grass.

I see.

For whosoever will save his life shall lose it: and whosoever will lose his life for my sake shall find it.
For what has a man profited, if he shall gain the whole world, and lose his own soul? Or what shall a man give in exchange for his own soul?

Matthew 16:25-26

Compassion

I will have compassion. I will look beyond the surface into what is really going on. Before I judge a person for their silliness or foibles, I will take time to wonder what got them where they are. If those I know have to prop themselves up on what seem like petty vanities, I will look a little further: I will try to imagine the inner emptiness of those who do not feel that who they are or what they have is enough. I will ask myself why it is that they feel the need to pretend, to pose, to hide who they really are. If they were truly confident of a situation, they would not have to push it in my face. If what they say they are were really theirs, they would simply be it. When I feel myself getting short-tempered, I will try to understand what they are really wanting from me but do not have the courage to ask. I will take an extra minute when I am feeling pressured by someone to wonder what lies behind it.

I will look with compassion.

If you see him riding on a bamboo cane, say to him, good health to your horse.

Moroccan proverb

May

Go placidly amid the noise and the haste, and remember what peace there may be in silence. As far as possible, without surrender, be on good terms with all persons. Speak your truth quietly and clearly; and listen to others, even to the dull and the ignorant; they too have their story. Avoid loud and aggressive persons; they are vexatious to the spirit. If you compare yourself with others, you may become vain or bitter, for always there will be greater and lesser persons than yourself.

Enjoy your achievements as well as your plans. Keep interested in your own career, however humble; it is a real possession in the changing fortunes of time. Exercise caution in your business affairs, for the world is full of trickery. But let this not blind you to what virtue there is; many persons strive for high ideals, and everywhere life is full of heroism.

Be yourself. Especially do not feign affection. Neither be cynical about love; for in the face of all aridity and disenchantment, it is as perennial as the grass. Take kindly the counsel of the years, gracefully surrendering the things of youth. Nurture strength of spirit to shield you in sudden misfortune. But do not distress yourself with dark imaginings. Many fears are born of fatigue and loneliness. Beyond a wholesome discipline, be gentle with yourself.

You are a child of the universe no less than the trees and the stars; you have a right to be here. And whether or not it is clear to you, no doubt the universe is unfolding as it should. Therefore be at peace with God, whatever you conceive Him to be. And whatever your labors and aspirations, in the noisy confusion of life, keep peace in your soul. With all its sham, drudgery and broken dreams, it is still a beautiful world. Be cheerful. Strive to be happy.

Max Ehrmann, "Desiderata"

Emotions

It is not necessarily emotions themselves, but rather, my relationship to them that creates problems for me. When I regard certain emotions as "good" and others as "bad," I erect inner barriers that prevent me from processing my feelings and understanding them. Sitting with my emotions and experiencing them allows them to be released and integrated into the energy of my self system. Their meaning can only become clear to me as I allow myself to experience them. When I label certain emotions as "bad," in a sense, I refuse to accept them. I disown them and think that by disowning them, they will disappear. Quite the contrary—the very process of disowning them increases their power. What I disown in myself, and find too painful to feel or accept as being a part of me, I oftentimes project outward onto someone else. This does not help me understand myself or another person and is fair to no one.

Today I will own my emotions.

Nothing vivifies and nothing kills like the emotions.

Joseph Roux

Overscheduling

I find that I often overschedule and overplan my life. The result is that I feel behind the eight ball. I feel stressed, as if I don't have time to do the things I like to do or see the people I want to see. My mental state grows pressured and somewhat agitated. This is cyclical. I do too much because I fear empty time. I get stressed out, forget to take care of myself and therefore feel empty inside—then I do too much again in an attempt not to feel empty or to calm my growing anxiety. When I feel this cycle getting engaged today, I will reassess. I will pause, calm down and remember that taking care of myself is an important priority. Part of taking care of myself is allowing myself time to rest and refuel. This gives soul time to enter my day. Taking good care of myself allows me to fill up from within and appreciate what I do and have, rather than what I have to do.

I can let go of excessive activity.

We are truly indefatigable in providing for the needs of the body, but we starve the soul.

Ellen Wood

▼

Challenge

I am up to the adventure of living a life with spirit and meaning, to the challenge of going within. I have to fight my battles within my own heart, to face my tigers in the night. Fear of my own inner void or emptiness is a primary fear. It keeps me tied to illusion and chasing false gods, rather than accepting my own inner void and living with and through it. Often I allow myself to be taken in by the false notion that there is something out there in the world that will solve my life, that will insure my happiness if only I can acquire it. This is not the life of soul—rather, it is the path away from soul.

I am willing to be challenged.

He was, first and last, the born fighter, to whom the consciousness of being matched against a great adversary suffices and who can dispense with success. Life for him was an adventure, perilous indeed, but men are not made for safe havens. The fullness of life is in the hazards of life. And, at the worst, there is that in us which can turn defeat into victory.

Edith Hamilton, referring to Aeschylus

▼

Living in an Ideal

I am surrounded by a quiet sort of beauty. A normal day has a quiet rhythm and grace. Living in an ideal is different from living in the moment. It makes me want to get the moment to conform to my idea of what it *should* be, and I miss the experience of what it is. What surrounds me has its own kind of meaning which I miss when I try to assign it a meaning that I wish it had or that I have decided it has to have in order for me to consider it important. What is important is what surrounds me right now, the simple pleasures that fill my mind and heart. The countless miracles that I encounter in the course of my day.

———————————— ▼ ————————————

Today I will let meaning emerge as it
wishes and I will just be there.

————————————————————————

Give me a look, give me a face
That makes simplicity a grace;
Robes loosely flowing, hair as free.
Such sweet neglect more taketh me
Than all the adulteries of art;
They strike mine eyes, but not my heart.

Ben Jonson

Letting Go

I will try to let go today. My fear of change keeps me from moving into further stages of living. I look around me and my life is good. But I forget that I participated in making it so. I have to constantly remind myself that I create my own experience of life, that a day will continue to present itself before me each time I wake up.

The attitude that I take toward my life is mine. No one can take it away from me unless I let them. Life takes courage; so does happiness. Often I abandon my own happiness because I am afraid that in taking a positive attitude, I am only tricking myself into feeling happy. But that is not happiness—it's just denial. Real happiness does not depend on denying pain. Real happiness accepts life as it is and enjoys it anyway—realizing that given the choice, one may as well relax and be amused by the ride, and stand in awe of the quiet and abiding mystery.

Happiness is an inside job.

Most people are about as happy as they make up their minds to be.

Mark Twain

▼

The Angle of Vision

It is the way I look at my life that determines my experience of it. I share the same world with millions of people. The same sun shines on all of us; we walk beneath the same sky. We all eat from one table. My day is in my intelligent hands. I co-create my life on a minute-to-minute basis. How I look at my life gets recorded into my brain as my life story because my life story is written by me. The wisdom and depth that I am able to bring to my life sit within me like a still pool of water over which my experience of the moment is reflected. From there I look at it, within the privacy of my own mind and heart, the quiet of my own soul.

▼

I see what I see.

What is life but the angle of vision? A man is measured by the angle at which he looks at objects. What is life but what a man is thinking of all day? This is his fate and his employer. Knowing is the measure of the man. But how much we know, so much we are.

Ralph Waldo Emerson

140

Authorization Within

Today I will spend time with soul. I will not run after life today; rather, I will let it unfold itself to me minute by minute throughout my day. I will anchor myself from within.

I will be the author of my own journey.

I call the high and light aspects of my being
spirit *and the dark and heavy aspects* soul.

Soul is at home in the deep, shaded valleys.
Heavy torpid flowers saturated with black grown there.
*   The rivers flow like*
warm-syrup. They empty into huge oceans of soul.

Spirit is a land of high, white peaks and glittering
*   jewel-like lakes and flowers.*
Life is sparse and sounds travel great distances.

There is soul music, soul food and soul love.

People need to climb the mountain not simply because it
*   is there but because*
the soulful divinity needs to be mated with the spirit.

Tenlin Gratso (14th-Century Dali Lama of Tibet)

A Life's Purpose

When I bring my energies to bear on a task at hand, I am exercising my will and my strength. I am bringing more of me out of hiding and into the arena of life. My palette of colors are the situations that present themselves to me in my day. Whatever those situations are, there is where my work lies, where my potential for soul growth is the greatest. When I retreat into the stillness within me, I am nourished by the purity of my own spirit, which is one with all that is infinite. The silence within me is the quivering silence of the universe, of all that was, is and will be. It is that space from which my potential for life issues.

▼

I will engage fully in the task at hand.

The gap is your connection to the field of pure potentiality. It is that state of pure awareness, that silent space between thoughts, that inner stillness that connects you to true power. And when you squeeze the gap, you squeeze your connection to the field of pure potentiality and infinite creativity.

Deepak Chopra

▼

Process vs. Goal

What is it about the process that is more alive than the capture of the goal? Perhaps it is the state of passive awareness that allows spontaneity to continually be experienced in the pursuit. I oftentimes define the goal, but do not as strictly define every moment of how I will go about achieving it. There is more room for chance and spontaneity on the road to the goal than in the holding and achieving of the goal itself.

"Life is what happens to you when you are making other plans." When I allow myself to live a day at a time, I am at the same time living with the constant recognition that I am not in charge of the blueprint. I am allowing God and chance and spontaneity to be a part of my day. I experience my own aliveness in the world in which I live. I will allow my goal to reveal itself to me one day at a time.

▼

I am enjoying the process.

We are involved in a life that passes understanding and our highest business is our daily life.

John Cage

143

▼

Becoming Real

My willingness to grapple with life, to struggle with relationships, to let people get under my skin makes me real.

▼

I am able to be real.

"Real isn't how you are made," said the Skin Horse. "It's a thing that happens to you. When a child loves you for a long, long time, not just to play with, but REALLY loves you, then you become Real." "Does it hurt?" asked the Rabbit. "Sometimes," said the Skin Horse, for he was always truthful. "When you are Real you don't mind being hurt." "Does it happen all at once, like being wound up," he asked, "or bit by bit?" "It doesn't happen all at once," said the Skin Horse. "You become. It takes a long time. That's why it doesn't often happen to people who break easily, or have sharp edges, or who have to be carefully kept. Generally, by the time you are Real, most of your hair has been loved off, and your eyes drop out and you get loose in the joints and very nappy. But these things don't matter at all, because once you are Real you can't be ugly, except to people who don't understand."

from the *Velveteen Rabbit*

I Belong Here

If I feel at times that I have no place I will remember that I am meant to be here. The universe planned on me; I am part of the pattern. My mind and my soul are a part of the All-mind and the All-soul. The tiny particles of truth, light and spirit that are contained within me are exactly the same as those contained within all other life.

I am part of life.

I think above all what I welcome is the sense that the mind is not just something existing in a vacuum playing on neutral items and trying to put them together into a theory but the mind itself belongs in things; it responds to what's there and vibrates in tune. One of the things the anthropic principle says is, this is a universe in which mind belongs; it is a natural part of the system. That means that this helps us with a sense of getting back into the universe after a couple of centuries when I think on the whole the ideal was of getting out of it, being nowhere in particular so you could see things from a privileged vantage point.

Rowan Williams

Being Divine

I will look within for my own soul. I will not wait to be told, sold, led or given permission to connect with my own individual soul. I will take my own opportunity to connect and that opportunity is *now!* Who owns the spirit? No one. Spirit and soul belong to everyone equally.

▼

I accept my fair share of the divine.

When science and religion see themselves as separate, they ask people to make a fundamental split within themselves between their spiritual selves and their physical selves. Splitting off in this way makes the world feel senseless and meaningless. It removes us from the inner belief that we are contained within an allied system, part of it, one with what it is intrinsically made up of. This point of view mortifies the flesh and glorifies the Divine, but gives us no sense of direct access to the Divine, that is, without an intermediary we are incapable of finding our own souls. The tragedy of this is that if we do not first look within ourselves for soul, we will never find it.

Matthew Fox

▼

Living with Paradox

When I justify myself and my position in life through anger and blame, I miss the opportunity to grow spiritually. I build a wall around myself for protection, but unfortunately, in keeping others out, I keep myself out as well. I get stuck in my rationalizations and use them to hide my own fears.

Fear is natural. No one gets through life without feeling plenty of it. Avoiding it is like trying to cross a river without getting wet. Instead, I will create a safe holding environment within myself, within which I can *experience* my fears and anxieties. When I do this, I am surprised at how quickly they lift. Feeling them in this way is ultimately more productive than the endless energy expended on trying to keep them from surfacing or showing.

▼

I am willing to be uncomfortable.

A pinch of fair, a pinch of foul.
And bad and good makes best of all;
Beware the moderated soul
That climbs no fractional inch to fall.

Elinor Wylie

▾

This World

This world is splendid enough for me today. Everywhere I look, there is splendor and magic. Where am I when I miss this, when I walk by this deep and quiet beauty without even noticing? Today I will consciously cultivate a state of mind that *sees*; an openness to life. I will do what I need to do by getting enough rest, good food, quiet and exercise so that I do not have to spend my life recuperating from the day before. I will take proper care of myself so that I can see and appreciate beauty. Ignoring myself is not selfless. I am as important as anyone else.

▾

I will look after myself.

If my soul could get away from this so-called prison, be granted all the list of attributes generally bestowed on spirits, my first ramble on spirit-wings would not be among the volcanoes of the moon. Nor should I follow the sunbeams to their sources in the sun. I should hover about the beauty of our own good star. And I should go to the very center of our globe and read the whole splendid page from the beginning.

John Muir

Forgiveness

Forgiveness is a process that happens over time.

It is tempting to stay stuck cycling within anger, generated by pain, or to become numb so that the pain will not be felt, or to go into denial and not admit to myself that I hurt. When I allow myself to feel a wound, I am taking my first step toward healing. Forgiveness and healing are intermingled. When I am more healed, I feel as if there is less to forgive. Hiding my wound makes me feel adamant about my need for retribution or apology. I see the other person as responsible for my pain. But whether or not they are responsible, the pain lives within me, and that is where it needs to heal. Forgiveness is more possible when I am able to engage in my own process of healing. Today I will have the courage to stop pretending that something doesn't hurt.

I will do the inner work
necessary to forgive.

Forgiveness is the answer to the child's dream of a miracle by which what is broken is made whole again, what is soiled is again made clean.

Dag Hammarskjöld

All Is Life

I am alive. Each thought that I think has life and energy. Each movement I make is part of a sea of movement. There is nothing dead in the universe. When I block my own flow of energy by downcast, negative thinking, the world appears wooden and lifeless. When I tune out of life rather than into it, I lose my connection to what it means to be alive; I see life as a burden rather than a gift. All it takes for me to feel good about being alive is tuning in and accepting that I am part of a living universe. When I let myself be nurtured by the abundance of this world, I learn to live with an open rather than a closed hand, to live generously, to love freely.

▼

I am life itself.

If there be sorrow
let it be for things undone . . .
undreamed, unrealized, unattained
to these add one:
Love withheld . . .
. . . restrained

Mari Evans

▼

Unity in Diversity

I recognize the soul in others. I look past the superficial qualities that seem to separate us. Though we are different on the surface, in education, looks, position and power, one thing within each of us is the same—our humanness. Some are more in touch with this than others. Those who are better humans perhaps are more fully aware of their own divine natures. When they can know this, their life means something—their humanness is an expression of the divine. These vehicles of body and mind are what we were given to search out our own lessons and to grow through life. I will be a better human today through being a better soul.

▼

I look past the surface.

If you have lived about, you have lost that sense of the absoluteness and the sanctity of the habits of your fellow-patriots which once made you so happy in the midst of them. You have seen that there are a great many patriae in the world, and that each of these is filled with excellent people.

Henry James

Living in the Moment

A day-at-a-time relationship with life acts as a deterrent to the scarcity principle taking over my life. The scarcity principle sees life as holding a limited amount of satisfying objects or experiences, and if one does not gobble them all down the same year, or stuff them into three weeks of living, they will be gone. That will be the end of all good things. The day-at-a-time way of living sees that one cannot be in two places at once or do everything there is to do. Setting priorities or doing only the amount of activity that is comfortable has no bearing on what will be available to me in the future. All it really means is that by the time the future comes, I will be able to be in it in the same way I am in the moment, and that I will not have burnt myself out with anxiety and worry. Living a day at a time is the only way I can enjoy what lies around me, what I already have.

▼

I am with the moment.

The desire for imaginary benefits often involves the loss of present blessings.

Aesop

▼

Personal Path

I am not in a position to judge another person's path. While people's hearts are open to soul, that energy will find them in a highly individualized manner. Just as each child needs to be parented according to his or her own needs, each person will be brought toward soul according to his or her own needs. How people arrive there is not my affair. Next time I have a strong desire to judge another person, I will relieve myself of that responsibility and leave that job to a loving God. I am busy enough finding my own way. Today I will allow myself and others space to learn and grow without the fear of harsh judgment.

▼

I will let each person have his
or her own experience.

God doeth not need
Either man's work or his own gifts; who best
Bear his mild yoke, they serve him best; his state
Is Kingly; thousands at his bidding speed,
And post o'er land and ocean without rest;
They also serve who only stand and wait.

John Milton

▼

Minute to Minute

When I drop down into myself, I drop down into life. There are layers of meaning and reality, and they are available to me if I want to experience them. When I treat ordinary events as if they were just fillers, as if they were not the real thing, I miss *my* life. When I learn to pay attention to my daily activities, I live my life consciously, learning from my experience.

▼

I will live today one minute at a time.

We all live in and are made of a sea of neurons alive and in motion at all times. We are crossing into unknown regions of understanding. We are going into the very small and the very large and to our surprise, the study of the very large and the study of the very small are the same thing. If one wants to attach religious significance to that, I think one can. That decision is for each person to make . . . but what we can say scientifically is that the early universe had a symmetry to it, a beauty to it, and that creation in the sense of space and time as we know it did come into existence at an epoch fifteen billion years ago.

David Schramm

▼

Anchoring

I will anchor my life in what cannot be seen. By going deep within myself, I will connect with the beyond and brush the hand of God. To realize deeper and deeper layers of consciousness is the work of a lifetime. It will keep me young and alive and in tune.

I am anchored from within.

Thus, self-realization is not a fashionable experiment but the highest task an individual can undertake. For himself, it means the possibility of an anchor in what is indestructible and imperishable, in the primordial nature of the objective psyche. By self-realization he returns to the eternal stream in which birth and death are only stations of passage and the meaning of life no longer resides in the ego. Towards others it raises up within him the tolerance and kindness that is only possible in those who have explored and consciously experienced their own darkest depths. Toward the collectivity, its special value is that it can offer society a fully responsible individual who knows the obligation of the particular to the general from his own most personal experience, the experience of his own psychic brutality.

J. Jacobi, *The Psychology of C. G. Jung*

▼

Self-Honesty

In order to attain peace of mind, I will need to let go of being defensive about my own weaknesses. This does not mean that I will "cast my pearls before swine" or open up to someone who is not able to be kind; only that I recognize that I am not perfect, nor is anyone else. If I am worried about criticism from others, how can they really hurt me if I accept who I am? If they say something that is true about me, so be it. If I don't feel it is true, I needn't take it into my heart; in fact, it may say more about them than me. I trust myself to discriminate. Self-honesty can let me balance from within instead of from without.

I take an honest look within.

If only there were evil people somewhere; insidiously committing evil deeds, and it were necessary only to separate them from the rest of us and destroy them. But the line dividing good and evil cuts through the heart of every human being. And who is willing to destroy a piece of his own heart?

Alexander Solzhenitzyn

The Light Within

I see soul as the center of my existence. At the center of my being and in the center of my heart there is light, love and divine spirit. I know and feel that I am tapped into an infinite source of spiritual energy. It allows me to see life as more than just a collection of random circumstances. When I turn my back on this energy of light, I live in relative darkness. Life seems meaningless and uninspired. It is light that gives definition, shape and form. It allows me to see the beauty that surrounds me.

I have divine light within me.

If one considers oneself or one's life as a wheel in which there are spokes and then there is a central hub, then in the life without the divine, the ego is that hub, and all the spokes, the relationships and the events that happen are important or unimportant insofar as they affect the ego. We're hurt, we're angry, we act. If one lives in the divine presence and displaces at the hub, his ego for God or for the Divine, then what happens to him is now related to that hub.

Rabbi Samuel Drexel

▼

Daily Worship

I am conscious of living with the divine. I need go nowhere special to access spiritual light and wisdom, to experience eternity. Each moment of my day is alive with spiritual energy because the particles carrying that energy are present in all that lives. I could not get away from this even if I wanted to. Whether or not I am aware of it, this truth still exists. If I wish to grow and learn spiritual lessons, I will start by paying attention to my thoughts, my feelings, the circumstances of my day and the state of my personal relationships.

My temple of worship is within me.

Normal life is compatible with supreme realization and . . . direct mystical contact with the Divine and can be sustained in any setting or activity. This is a revolution, for it dissolves all dogmas and hierarchies, all separations between ordinary and spiritual life, sacred and profane, humdrum and mystical. A new spiritual age has dawned for humankind, an age in which the Divine will be present intimately, normally, consciously in all things and activities.

Andrew Harvey

Ritual

Rituals help me to access personal and universal meaning through the use of symbol and metaphor. I need this meaning, this device through which I can make order out of chaos or sense out of apparent senselessness, in order to give voice to my human experience and to ground my inner world in a larger context. Ritual is the language of the collective and the individual soul. It calls forth truth and meaning and links the ordinary experience of day-to-day living with the transcendent life of the soul.

I respect ritual in my life.

Upon reflection, is it not odd that human beings, in all societies, everywhere and in all ages, have engaged in the making and performing of rituals. Why have they done this, when life is full of dangers and challenges that would seem to require more practical kind of activity? . . . they seem to be born out of necessity . . . and the people who best know that life is difficult are the ones most likely to cleave to ritual and make it work for them.

Tom F. Driver

Personal Power

There is no separating myself from reality. I am not an objective pair of eyes that has no effect on my surroundings. I am powerful and my effect on a situation is also significant. When I do not own my own power, my read on life is always slightly distorted because I leave me out. I tell myself that I am being objective but I am, in truth, never objective, I am always subjective. When I try to understand a situation as if I were not in it, I haven't a prayer of really understanding it. In order for an interaction to make sense, I need to take my own actions into account, to be willing to understand my own impact.

I count myself in.

We cannot withdraw our cards from the game. Were we as silent and as mute as stories, our very passivity would be an act.

Jean-Paul Sartre

▼

Thinking and Doing

I will pay attention to the contents of my thoughts. Even when I do not give voice to them, they are felt by others as nonverbal messages. What I think is more powerful than I care to admit. The thoughts I think exist in living tissue and move through and beyond me. They become a part of the creative substance of life. They take a shape, they have an impact. I will try to live peacefully today with the heart of the universe. Life is a journey, my day is a part of that journey. I see myself as a traveler moving through the world knowing I am not here forever, I am here to experience where I am. I will observe my thoughts and my actions and see how they affect my life.

▼

I observe what I do and what I think.

Oh my brothers, God exists. There is a soul at the center of nature and over the will of every man, so that none of us can wrong the universe. Besides, why should we be cowed by the name of Action? 'Tis a trick of the senses, no more. We know that the ancestor of every action is a thought . . . to think is to act.

Ralph Waldo Emerson

Centering Within the Self

I will not walk by the mysteries that surround me as if they did not exist. The modern world in which I live and spend my time deadens me to the beauty and the mystery of life. There is mystery and beauty everywhere I look. When I can appreciate this, my world is transformed from a cold and wooden collection of objects to a place teeming with life. When I lose myself in sensory overload I do just that—I lose myself, my inner center, my soul awareness. This world offers me endless distractions, endless hallways down which to get lost. There is only one place to be found, and that's by turning within and enhancing my true connection with self and soul. Only then can I keep the things of the world in perspective, enjoying them for what they can give me, yet not looking to them for what they cannot. It is through the self that I connect with life. The Kingdom of Heaven is within me, the Kingdom of Soul is at hand.

I establish a home within the self.

We are more curious about the meaning of dreams than about things we see when awake.

Diogenes

Non-Attachment

I will practice non-attachment in the affairs of my day today. Non-attachment acts as a deterrent to my co-dependent relationship with the people, places and things of my day. When thoughts go through my mind, I will let them do just that, go through. I do not have to mentally chase after every thought. When I do that, I can get lost in a sort of circular reasoning or compulsive ruminating that is not productive.

I have choices. I can choose which thoughts to dwell on and which to let pass by. When I can practice non-attachment in my mind, I can begin to practice it in the activities of my day. I will allow myself to choose how and when to get involved. I will observe from a place of non-attachment that allows me to be free and serene.

I am centered from within.

Approach it and there is no beginning;
follow it and there is no end.
You can't know it, but you can be it,
at ease in your own life.

Lao Tzu

Recognition and Reverence

Reverence for the life of the soul is all encompassing. To revere all of life is to recognize that soul is contained therein. All concrete life, all human interaction, all that breathes with life is holy. When I look for the life and the energy of my soul, I will look to the small events and interactions of my day-to-day life. Finding soul means recognizing soul, allowing soul to be present and not denying and suppressing its coming forth.

I recognize soul's constant presence.

The great fault of all ethics hitherto has been that they believed themselves to have to deal only with the relations of man to man. In reality . . . the question is what is his attitude to the world and all life that comes within his reach. A man is ethical only when life . . . is sacred to him . . . and when he devotes himself helpfully to all life that is in need of help. Only the universal ethic . . . can be founded in thought. The ethic of Reverence for Life, therefore, comprehends within itself everything that can be described as love, devotion, and sympathy whether in suffering, joy, or effort.

Albert Schweitzer

164

▼

Attachment to the Familiar

My attachment to what is familiar can keep me from moving forward in my life. Moving into new areas of experience necessitates experimenting with and recombining the known. If I want to swim in the water, I have to leave the security of the diving board. My soul expresses itself through me; anything that I can do to unblock and open my channels of creativity and productivity allows soul to come through more fully. It is fear that stands in my way—not only fear of the unknown, but also fear of loss. Even if I *want* to move through and beyond a stage or circumstance of my life, moving beyond is still a loss of the known. Today I will put my faith in the unseen. I trust that God will take care of me if I am willing to take a risk, to make a move toward more of me.

▼

I am willing to lose something
that feels familiar.

All changes, even the most longed for, have their melancholy, for what we leave behind us is a part of ourselves; we must die to one life because we can enter into another.

Anatole France

165

June

love is a place
& through this place of
love move
(with brightness of peace)
all places

yes is a world
& in this world of
yes live
(skillfully curled)
all worlds

e. e. cummings

The Process of Healing

I am in a constant state of healing. I will not get it right once and for all and finally be healed. I will be aware of what part of me is healing today.

I open to deep healing.

Some part of us is always in the process of healing . . . the condition of health is not a static state of perfect wellness; it is . . . a condition of ongoing healing. For example, a possible explanation for the cause of cancer is referred to as the "scanner theory." This theory holds that various cells in the healthy body routinely become cancerous; but the body remains healthy because within it there is some . . . mechanism that scans the body for such malignant cells . . . and proceeds to kill them before they multiply into a growing tumor. What causes cancer then, according to the theory, is not a cancerous cell but rather the failure of the "scanner" to detect it. . . . The theory is offered not because it is proven, but because it demonstrates the way in which physicians are increasingly coming to think about disease: that most disease may best be defined as a failure of the healing process.

M. Scott Peck, M.D.

Soul's Unfolding

I get out of my own way, so that I can experience deeper layers of self. I can tolerate stillness. All that I need do in order to have a soul experience is to be still and await seeing the table prepared before me. I have a choice. I can turn my back on spirit or I can turn my eyes toward it. Soul is always present, always alive and in the moment, patiently waiting to be seen and known. Actually, it is not even patient: it simply is. I am the one for whom patience is an issue, who is constantly preoccupied and not paying attention. Today I will remember to be still. Each time that I am still is money in the bank of soul. I can draw on it throughout my day when I need it.

▼

I will be still with my soul
and feel it unfold.

You do not leave your room. Remain sitting at your table and listen. Do not even listen, simply wait. Do not even wait. Be quite still and solitary. The world will freely offer itself to you to be unmasked, it has no choice, and it will roll in ecstasy at your feet.

Franz Kafka

▼

A Quiet Prayer

I say a quiet prayer for those I love. I know that my prayers have power. The prayer that I hold in my heart for another person is held in both our hearts. It is helped by invisible hands, blown by the breath of angels toward the soul of another. Love leads one toward what is right and good in this life. If I can love, the rest will fall into place. This love that I feel will teach and guide me, it will give me courage to act or to temper my aggression. It is this experience of love that is the single most important part of my life. Through love all else will come, all is possible.

▼

All things remain in love.

W. B. Yeats

May the road rise to meet you,
May the wind be always at your back
May the sun shine warm upon your face,
May the rain fall soft upon your fields,
And, until we meet again,
May God hold you in the palm of his hand.

Irish blessing

A Different Kind of Fullness

I am an organic part of this happening called life. It is inescapable, I am one with it, a part of it, real and alive. All that I see around me and feel within me is life repeating itself in vast and wondrous variety. There is nothing but what is real, nothing but what is alive. There are no gaps, no breaks, no empty spots. When I recognize this, I fill up. It is that simple. If all is life, then empty is still alive, empty becomes full. Real also has wondrous variety. It is not walking away; rather, it is staying with it—whether the *it* be a feeling, a person or a moment in time. Real is being in my own skin and experiencing the moment. Being real is not leaving but staying with life.

I am willing to stay with it.

If it were possible to talk to the unborn, one could never explain to them how it feels to be alive, for life is washed in the speechless real.

Jacques Barzun

▼

A Course Toward Soul

I will set my course toward soul today. I am not looking for a quick fix or a spiritual awakening that will change my life in the length of an hour. I am not hoping to be reborn by midnight. Rather, I am altering my course to tack toward soul. When I learn to navigate the changing waters of my life, to ride out the storms and relish the calm, I will be naturally moving toward my goal just through the act of living. The trick is to head in the right direction. When I do that, my focus allows the solving of day-to-day situations and issues to bring me closer to where I am ultimately aimed. Time is just the illusion of heading in the direction of soul. Soul is a direction, an experience, not a place. It allows me to resolve all that is in the way, as long as I hold a steady course, as long as I stay in the boat.

▼

This is the soul moment.

If I lose my direction, I have to look for the North Star, and I go to the north. That does not mean I expect to arrive at the North Star. I just want to go in that direction.

Thich Nhat Hanh

Self-Study

I commit myself to a life truly examined. Living in this manner is not necessarily popular. I may appear to others as if I devote too much attention to detail, too much time spent on thinking about life. But what is more important than coming closer to the meaning of life, or learning the art of living well? When I do not look deeply into my own life with honesty and intelligence, I lose the opportunity to study in my own laboratory.

I am all that I have. I learn about myself through witnessing myself in action, through examining my inner and outer being at work. Learning to be a true observer of myself teaches me how to study others. Scholarly self-study is truly what makes me a philosopher of life. Studying myself is studying all people because all of us have the same origin. To study myself is to study life and God and the universe.

▼

I embark on a sincere course of self-study.

The unexamined life is not worth living.

Socrates

Dispassionate Observation

When I gain detachment from my own thinking process, I am able to be separate from my own obsessive and neurotic thinking. I can watch my thoughts in a dispassionate manner. I can be a witness to my own emotional and mental processes. When I cultivate this habit of mind, I am provided with a wonderful opportunity to learn about what makes me tick. Getting lost in every thought I have leads me away from self. There is no greater teacher than that of my own internal witness. When I look at the way in which I think, I can begin to self-define; to separate from who I have been programmed to be and make choices as to who I wish to become.

I witness my thought process.

We dis-identify by observing. Instead of being absorbed by sensations, feelings, desires, thoughts, we observe them objectively without judging them, without interfering with them in any way. We see them as distinct from us, as if we were looking at a landscape. We calmly observe these psychic arabesques from a detached viewpoint.

Piero Ferrucci

The Cradle of the Mysterious

All truth and beauty issue from the mysterious. When I tune into the mysteries of human and natural life, I am also contemplating the mysteries of life, time, matter and energy, I am moving my spirit toward creation. I am nourished on every level by my quiet contemplation of the infinite, wherever and however I choose to make contact. Moving toward the source of all life renews my spirit and makes faith not only a leap but an actual experience. I will remember the importance of quiet contemplative time in my day today. Time to be, to tune in, to be still and nourished from the well of wisdom within me. Time to remember and be part of the mystery.

I take time to contemplate the mystery.

The most beautiful experience we can have is the mysterious. It is the fundamental emotion which stands at the cradle of true art and true science. Whosoever does not know it and can no longer wonder, no longer marvel, is as good as dead, and his eyes are dimmed.

Albert Einstein

Involved with Life

I will allow myself to attend to and take pleasure in every detail of my day. When I take interest in the activities of my day, I experience it differently. Instead of managing my day, I live it. Rather than seeing my day as a series of tasks to be accomplished, I am able to go with the flow of activity.

I am moved along by invisible helping hands.

Happiness is not something that happens. It is not the result of good fortune or random chance. It is not something that money can buy or power command. It does not depend on outside events, but, rather, on how we interpret them. Happiness, in fact, is a condition that must be prepared for, cultivated, and defended privately by each person. People who learn to control inner experience will be able to determine the quality of their lives, which is as close as any of us can come to being happy. Yet we cannot reach happiness by consciously searching for it. "Ask yourself whether you are happy," said J. S. Mill, "and you cease to be so." It is by being fully involved with every detail of our lives, whether good or bad, that we find happiness, not by trying to look for it directly.

Mitaly Csikszentmihalyi

Commitment

Oftentimes we think that if we can only choose just the right person, profession or town, we will be happy. But in truth, it is how well we relate to and take care of what we have that will ultimately matter. We are often better off working with what we have and making it right for us than spending our lives searching for our vision of perfection. In order for a relationship to deepen, be it with the self, another person or a life's work, commitment is necessary. Without it, we do not stay to work through the tough stuff. When things get painful or scary or confusing, we leave. Unfortunately, all too often we leave with our confusion and our load of pain still within us. Clarity comes in the working through of fear and hurt. This is one of the ways toward greater soul awareness—using issues that are activated within the self as we penetrate deeper layers of a relationship or a committed work.

I can hang in for one more day.

Life is a succession of lessons which must be lived in order to be understood.

Ralph Waldo Emerson

Being A Contender

Today I am a contender. Whatever the outcome of this race, I have shown that I have what it takes to be a winner. No matter what happens around me, I will use the noise, the chaos, the tension to spur me on into greater aspects of myself. Neck and neck for me is just a barometer of what's out there, triggering in me the excitement for movement, for risking and reaching. Today I will experience the vitality that issues from the one, the energy that is living, the wonders of the race. I am here and it is enough. It's good to be alive. It's good to be a contender.

I am already a winner.

No man is an island, entire of itself; every man is a piece of the continent, a part of the main. If a clod be washed away by the sea, Europe is the less, as well as if a promontory were, as well as if a manor of thy friend's or of thine own were: any man's death diminishes me, because I am involved in mankind, and therefore never seek to know for whom the bell tolls, it tolls for thee.

John Donne

▼

Co-Creating a Culture

Anyone can say that the world is going to hell in a handbasket. Not anyone can rise to the challenge of cherishing a world that needs love. We are now living in the global village predicted by Marshall McLuhan, learning what it means to live in a multicultural society, hungry for developing cultural rituals and mythology. We are writing our own story, co-creating a culture. The ideals and the values we are evolving today will impact many generations because we are placed at such a time in our cultural history when we are called upon to form an identity as a society. This evidences itself in a variety of ordinary ways: in the surging interest in architectural style and preservation, in ethnic food varieties, in our desire to explore a personal and cultural mythology, and an impassioned drive to look for self, soul and meaning. We are culture makers. Not only are these drives toward self and social actualization strong because we are lost, but also because we are beginning to be found.

▼

I will do my part to co-create my culture.

A baby is God's opinion that life should go on.

Carl Sandburg

Success

I will not make success my goal today or measure my state of happiness by it. If I am to succeed, it will be a byproduct of following a path that feels relevant and meaningful to me. I will try to follow my heart and respond to an impulse or a call from within. When I move in a direction that is natural for me, that draws and speaks to me, I have more of myself to bring to my work. Success will come to me naturally if I love what I do. Loving what I do is its own reward and will give me the staying power necessary to do well. It will help provide the motivation necessary to go the extra mile. Following my heart, my bliss, will put me on a track toward the realization of my soul's passion.

I will self-actualize through
following my heart.

Don't aim at success—the more you aim at it and make it a target, the more you are going to miss it. For success, like happiness, cannot be pursued; it must ensue . . . as the unintended side-effect of one's personal dedication to a course greater than oneself.

Viktor E. Frankl

Growing Anew

I become new—I grow young. As long as I have eyes to see and ears to hear, as long as my senses are alive, I am here. I have another chance at life.

I will learn something new today or take a fresh look at an existing situation. The same old information represented in a new way fosters cell growth in my brain; new connections are made and I learn. When I do this I actually help ward off the degenerative diseases connected with aging. I will walk into this day with a virgin sensibility. I will allow myself to be surprised and amazed.

I have not passed this way before.

As long as new perceptions continue to enter your brain, your body can respond in new ways. There is no secret of youth more powerful. As one 80-year-old patient of mine succinctly put it, "People don't grow old. When they stop growing, they become old." New knowledge, new skills, new ways of looking at the world keep mind and body growing, and as long as that happens, the natural tendency to be new at every second is expressed.

Deepak Chopra

▼

Dreaming

Dreaming dreams is how I co-author my life with divine providence. I will write a page in my own life today. I will take a moment to remember what my favorite fairy tales from childhood were. I will ask my heart what they meant to me, what about them applied to my own life, what I was trying to understand about myself or my hopes and dreams through them. Have I let myself have my own dreams?

▼

I will remember.

Fairy tales, unlike any other form of literature, direct the child to discover his identity and calling, and they also suggest what experiences are needed to develop his character further. Fairy tales intimate that a rewarding, good life is within one's reach despite adversity— but only if one does not shy away from the hazardous struggles without which one can never achieve true identity. These stories promise that if a child dares to engage in this fearsome and taxing search, benevolent powers will come to his aid, and he will succeed.

Bruno Bettleheim

▼

My Own Life

Today I will live my *own* life. Only when I am centered from within do I function in a coherent and coordinated way. This type of inner cohesion allows soul to come forth and be manifested through me. Divine energy is layered upon and laced through the illusion that surrounds me. When I live my own life, all the energies necessary to coordinate my day have a center of operation. I am living in my own skin, my reactions and interactions are in sync with who I am. I need to own what goes on in my life and work with it, to see my life as my own and to understand that it is mine to shape and give meaning to. When I live outside of myself, I lose access to my source of security and groundedness—I lose touch with my center. I am like a transistor—my life signals are monitored through my own living being.

▼

I live centered within my own life.

You need to claim the events of your life to make your life yours.

Ann Wilson-Schaef

The Laboratory of Soul Growth

John Keats said "call the world, if you please, the vale of soulmaking." Life is a laboratory for soul growth; the day-to-day situations and circumstances that we encounter are the means through which we investigate the deeper truths of life, grist for the mill of soulmaking. When we learn to use everyday life as our personal journey toward self and soul, we grow gradually toward a higher state of consciousness and a more meaningful existence. I will use the physical and psychological situations in my life as vehicles for soul growth. I will use the circumstances of my life as my personal journal of soulmaking, my path toward my own individual soul. The world is a puzzle waiting to be solved, ever presenting new and complicated situations for me to work and grow through. I recognize that my life is a workbook that I address at my own rate.

My life is my schoolroom for soulmaking.

Man is born a child, his power is the power of youth.

Rabindranath Tagore

Context

I live in a context. What I learn has meaning vis-á-vis the context in which it happens. I will not judge myself or others out of context. I am not independent of my surroundings; I am a part of them and they of me. The way that I handle my self in my life is part of how I learn and stretch the limits of my knowledge and an expression of my particular kind of intelligence. When I confine my idea of intelligence to one or two types, I cheat myself out of feeling smart and owning my competence and strength. Each person, each culture has its own uniqueness, its own special gifts, its own way of being intelligent.

▼

I recognize many forms of intelligence.

Beyond the years of early childhood, human accomplishment presupposes an awareness of the different domains of knowledge in one's culture and the various "field forces" that affect opportunity, progress, and recognition. By focusing on the knowledge that resides within a single mind at a single moment, formal testing may distort, magnify, or grossly underestimate the contributions that an individual can make within a larger social setting.

Howard Gardner

▼

Making Mistakes

I am human. I make mistakes. Sometimes when I make a mistake I catastrophize it and soon I feel myself to be a really bad person. Once this gets going, I worry that others will see me as bad. I fear that they see me in the way that I am seeing me. The self-condemnation is now complete, and I have successfully worked myself into a hole. My sense of failure keeps me going back and forth between shame and blame. I have trouble breaking free and letting go of my negative self-image. But mistakes are only meant for me to learn from. If I have hurt someone, I need to make amends and let go. If I have made an error, I need to correct it, at least in myself, and move on. If I can't correct it, I can learn from it, enrich my spirit and release it.

▼

I am allowed to make mistakes.

For the wonderful thing about saints is that they were human. They lost their tempers, got angry, scolded God, were egotistical or testy or impatient in their turns, made mistakes and regretted them. Still they went on doggedly blundering toward heaven.

Phyllis McGinley

▼

Paradigm Shift

Seeing soul as a part of all that is living may require me to make a paradigm shift—a shift in perception, a new inner construction. It may not be so much an accumulation of new knowledge as a change in the way I *see*. Seeing the world as alive and teeming with soul and spirit is a shift in consciousness or a change in the way I am used to understanding things. The way that I perceive the world need not be fixed. After all, before Columbus, many people really did think the world was flat.

▼

I am willing to see things differently.

The word paradigm *comes from the Greek. . . . In the more general sense, it's the way we "see" the world—not in terms of our visual sense of sight, but in terms of perceiving, understanding, interpreting.*

For our purposes, a simple way to understand paradigms is to see them as maps. We all know that "the map is not the territory." A map is simply an explanation of certain aspects of the territory. That's exactly what a paradigm is. It is a theory, an explanation, or model of something else.

Stephen R. Covey

Depression and Self-Esteem

Depression has long been seen as caused in part by unfelt pain or anger that we are unable to express for one reason or another and so turn inward onto ourselves. If anger and pain go unfelt and unexpressed over a long period of time, they drag on the spirit and depress it.

Learning to feel anger and do constructive things about it helps to build self-esteem, and self-esteem helps to reduce anger. On the other hand, escaping anger by acting out, yelling, screaming, hitting, or being violent tends to reduce self-esteem. It is at best a temporary relief, but it is borne out of a person who is feeling bad about herself. Acting out the anger makes me feel worse about myself. I feel ashamed of my out-of-control actions but may be unable to admit that shame to myself or others. Consequently, to avoid feeling the shame, I continue to act out the anger and hurt in destructive way.

I can feel pain and anger.

No man is angry that feels not himself hurt.

Francis Bacon

Surrender

The internal position of surrender is a recognition that I am not in control of every event or circumstance of my life. It is a chosen sense of powerlessness, it frees me from my illusion of control. The take-charge person knows how to work with the natural flow of events and personalities in order to accomplish something; letting providence and individual creativity play a role. The controlling person attempts to manipulate people and situations to conform to her idea of what is right. This person shuts down the creative possibilities.

I let go and let God.

The concept of surrender runs contrary to the Western mind. We have been taught to aggressively go after what we want, to make things happen. But surrender asks us to allow events to unfold at their own pace, to get out of our own way and to let go of our desire for control. Surrender is an act of trust in the universe, an acknowledgment that there are forces beyond our own will at work. Most people ask for happiness on condition. Happiness can only be felt if you don't set any condition.

Arthur Rubenstein

▼

Living in Spirit

When I think I am only a body, I am in denial of
my true source of aliveness. When I think I am only a
soul, I forget to be human. I am in this body for a purpose, so that I can further actualize and move toward
soul. Soul is not about being a goody-goody, or not
making mistakes or never hurting—it's about being
alive. There is nowhere to hide from life. I can become
numb or deny it, but that only leaves me listless and
depressed and makes life feel meaningless. Why not
go with the flow? Why not let God happen?

▼

I embrace my spirit nature.

The question whether soul and body are identical, there-
fore, is as superfluous as to ask whether wax and the
shape imprinted on it are identical, or, in general
whether the material of a thing is identical with the
thing of which it is the material. "Is" and "one" have
various meanings, but in their most legitimate meaning
they connote the fully actual character of a thing.

Aristotle

The Burden of the World

Today I will release myself from the burdens of the world, of taking what I see and do so seriously that I neglect and forget what is really important. When I see only the world and forget my essential divine nature, life hangs on me like a heavy cloak. I will remind myself that though I am in this world, I am also with God.

I remember my divine nature.

The World is too much with us; late and soon.
Getting and spending, we lay waste our powers,
Little we see in Nature that is ours;
We have given our hearts away, a sordid boon!
This sea that bares her bosom to the moon;
The winds that will be howling at all hours,
And are up-gathered now like sleeping flowers;
For this, for everything, we are out of tune;
It moves us not—Great God! I'd rather be
A Pagan suckled in a creed outworn,
So might I, standing on this pleasant lea,
Have glimpses that would make me less forlorn;
Have sight of Proteus rising from the sea,
Or hear old Triton blow his wreathed horn.

William Wordsworth

▼

An Attitude of Healing

It was Viktor E. Frankl who said that the only thing that we have that cannot be taken away from us are our attitudes, the contents of our minds and hearts. Today, more than ever, we are called upon to take an attitude that will promote wellness and healing, to choose life. When I take responsibility for the contents of my mind and heart, I take my place as a person of value to society. Quantum physics tells me that we are all part of the same particle mass, interconnected, of one stuff or soul. Who I am from within affects all that is without.

One very practical thing that I can do for my world is to think positively about it. I can attempt to live a more conscious life. Each person who transforms within, who enters into this struggle toward a more conscious life brings others with them.

▼

I will live consciously today.

---

and if i ever touched a life, i hope that life knows, that i know, that touching was is and always will be the only true revolution.

nikki giovanni

▼

Getting to Know Myself

Getting to know myself is my most rewarding and powerful adventure, my God story. It is a day-to-day task, it does not happen once and for all because the self evolves. Today I will try to get out of my own way and allow the deeper pulse of life and love and spiritual energy to flow through me. I often attempt to rid my personality of what I perceive to be undesirable aspects, to get them out of me once and for all. But today I wonder if rather than get rid of parts of myself, perhaps I need to learn to work with these troublesome areas and reintegrate them in a new way. It need not be my goal today to get rid of pieces of myself I dislike, but instead to work with them and transform them into something better through attention, care, self-honesty and self-forgiveness. I get more done with a loving and caring attitude toward others—why not try to be loving and caring with myself?

▼

I will work and live with all of me.

There is a land of the living and a land of the dead and the bridge is love, the only survival, the only meaning.

Thornton Wilder

Hatred

Pretending that painful or negative feelings do not exist doesn't keep relationships more intimate. It can even create inner distance when I act as if the intimate relationship is not strong enough to hold pain, anger or hate. Powerful feelings can be frightening, but denying their presence keeps me from deeper layers of self. When my intimate relationships are able to hold the powerful, paradoxical feelings of love and hate, anger and forgiveness, something deep within me can relax and let go. If they are not able to do this, I need to withdraw from the relationship in order to be myself.

I can hold angst.

In this era of self-understanding and conscious efforts at parenting, we learn we should not come down to our children's level. That is, we should not be as hateful toward them as they are to us. Yet, if we seal ourselves off they are cheated and burdened by the illusion that anger and hatred are personally inappropriate. Therapists are like parents. When the therapist comes down to their level, both grow from it when the generation gap is reestablished.

David V. Keith

▼

A Dream and Faith

I will take stock of my life today. I will do some small thing to make my day a little bit more beautiful and positive. I only need to do a little better. I don't need to reach for the moon or to become perfect. If I don't hold a good dream for myself and this world, who will? It is up to me as much as anyone else. If I don't have faith in humanity, who will? It is my responsibility to help God. My spirituality and my inner relationship with soul guide me. They show me daily where to look to see light. They let me know that my efforts are worthwhile. I will dream a little dream today. I will think up something—some good work, whether it be planting a tree or helping to build a program. I will make a contribution. Rather than complain about what isn't here that I want, I will take steps to create it.

▼

I will plant a garden.

All we need to begin with is a dream that we can do better than before. All we need to have is faith, and that dream will come true. All we need to do is act, and the time for action is now.

Carl Sandburg

Being in Touch

In a search for God and a search for self, I always end up coming home. Dorothy from *The Wizard of Oz*, when asked by Glenda what she learned on her journey, replied, "I learned that if I ever lose my heart's desire again, I won't go looking past my own backyard because if it isn't there, I never really lost it to begin with." Dorothy's search for the wizard ended in the discovery that he was only a man behind a curtain, with all the needs and frailties that she, herself, had.

I can make my journey endless by seeking God or self outside of me in people, places and things, or I can shorten it by turning inward and looking for them where I am most likely to find them. Exactly how I get there is of little import. Ultimately the path will fade away behind me, anyway. It is the being there that matters; my willingness to know that my search begins and ends in the same place, within me.

I am the man behind and in
front of the curtain.

This is the grand atonement, the being in touch.

D. H. Lawrence

▼

Accepting My Limitations

True connection with others also requires connection with self. When I look toward connection with others to fill my lonely emptiness, I never get what I want. I become a perfectionist and demanding because I see what the other is giving as crucial to my personal sense of wellness. Within me is a fullness from which I can have a true encounter with the fullness of another person. Two empty containers don't make one full one. Today I will go within for nourishment and support another person in doing the same. When each of us is able to do this, we will have something beautiful to share.

▼

I connect with the fullness of others
through the fullness of my own soul.

Soul or saint making is not an overnight process; it may take most of our lives, or it may take only a few revelations of the truth—it all depends on who we are and what we are dealing with. That is why it is so important to have respect for one another. Finding the gifts at the core of our soul is an interesting process. It frees us to be truly ourselves in the most beautiful light available, God's love.

Terry Lynn Taylor

July

To every thing there is a season, and a
time to every purpose under the
heaven:

A time to be born, and a time to die; a
time to plant, and a time to pluck up
that which is planted;

A time to kill, and a time to heal; a time to
break down, and a time to build up;

A time to weep, and a time to laugh; a
time to mourn, and a time to dance;

A time to cast away stones, and a time to
    gather stones together; a time to
    embrace, and a time to refrain from
    embracing;
A time to get, and a time to lose; a time
    to keep, and a time to cast away;
A time to rend, and a time to sew; a time
    to keep silence, and a time to speak;
A time to love, and a time to hate; a time
    of war, and a time of peace.

Ecclesiastes 3:-8

Toxicity and Pain

All learning is a process of paring down and building up brain cells. When I repress a memory, it lives in my brain as a cell assembly, with associations and feelings attached to it. When it becomes conscious and the full assembly comes to light, I can look at it in its entirety: I can see it with new eyes.

Inner growth can be seen as a shift in perception. Carl Jung says that we never really solve a problem, we simply go to the top of a mountain and learn to see the situation differently. These shifts in perception create shifts in self-concept and in the way I live my life. Each day I die a little and am reborn.

I experience a shift in perception.

Nay, but as when one layeth
His worn-out robes away,
And, taking new ones, sayeth,
"These will I wear to-day!"
So putteth by the spirit
Lightly its garb of flesh,
And passeth to inherit
A resident afresh.

The Song Celestial of Bhagavad-Gita

Friendship

I will value the comfort of friendship and hold a true friend dear. Soul is expressed through human relationship; care of relationships is care of the soul. Relationships are what trigger my anxieties. Intimacy acts like a black light under which my emotional cracks show up. In a close friendship I have an opportunity to see and feel those cracks, to allow them to be looked at so that I can work with them and heal. A friend is someone with whom I can explore my limits and become more of me.

I value friendship in my life.

Friendship is the comfort, the inexpressible comfort of feeling safe with a person, having neither to weigh thoughts nor measure words, but pouring all right out just as they are, chaff and grain together, certain that a faithful, friendly hand will take and sift them, keep what is worth keeping and with a breath of comfort, blow the rest away.

George Eliot

Trauma

When we are traumatized, we have one or more of the following responses: (1) fight (aggression), (2) flight (physically or psychologically leaving), or (3) freeze (becoming numb). Any of these responses preclude the normal working through of a situation by experiencing and confronting it, assessing options and making choices. When life experiences are not "lived through," they are stored in an unfinished state, absent of adequate closure. It is as if they are stored in suspension without the context that accompanies normal experience. When events are stored by the brain in this manner, they become part of our storehouse of "unfinished business." They form what comes to be the root of a hunger that cries out for action or completion. Today if I see myself acting out impulsively, I will ask myself what wound is trying to be heard and seen. Rather than continue to act out, I will quiet down and listen.

I am willing to know.

God gives, but man must open his hand.

German proverb

▼

A Full Human Being

I am willing to pay the price of personal and spiritual growth. Confronting the situations both within and outside that frighten me is not easy—it can feel terrifying, sometimes almost life-threatening. But today, rather than bemoan my fate, I will reach deep down into myself and look for something good. I will be sustained not only by courage but by a sort of goodness, a trust in life, a willingness to think that if I stay with it long enough and well enough, things will work out. I could give up on living fully, but I feel that if I did, I would regret it. Trouble and suffering are a part of the human condition. Once I accept that I am in a position to look for my rewards where they are most likely to be found—not in the world but in my relationship to it—I can move closer to spiritual living.

▼

I have a loving relationship with living.

Teach me, like you, to drink creation whole
And, casting out, my self, become a soul.

Richard Wilbur

Nirvana

The soul experience has many layers. Once I solve and comprehend one layer, another presents itself to me. The self, though fundamentally of one stuff, has countless manifestations. There is no part of me that I cannot use to better know myself. In fact, I must know all of me, invite all of myself into view in order to mature, grow and become fully human. I am in a position to move more easily beyond my smaller self into higher states of consciousness when I am not being pulled on and held back by my own hidden parts.

I look for peace in many places.

Nirvana removes the craving for further becoming, the craving for the cessation of becoming. Finally, Nirvana and medicine both give security—And these are the ten qualities which Nirvana shares with space. Neither is born, grows old, dies, passes away, or is reborn; both are unconquerable, cannot be stolen, are unsupported, are a road respectively for birds and Arhats to journey on, are unobstructed and infinite—Like the wishing jewel, Nirvana grants all one can desire, brings joy, and sheds light.

from Buddhist Scriptures

▼

Panic

I will work with my feelings of panic today. Rather than swing into emotional action by shutting the feeling down or by projecting my own panicky feeling onto someone else, I will first identify it as a feeling within me. When I project the feeling, I do not experience it. Then I do to another person what I am doing to myself. I distance myself from the emotions that make me uncomfortable in order to manage my anxiety. Why not try something different? When I experience the feeling of panic that makes me want to run from or shut off a particular emotion, rather than try to get rid of the feeling, I can allow myself to be with it, to explore it, to look at it from a variety of angles. In this way I can use my emotional problems for spiritual growth. I have the strength to sit with and move through my panicky feelings. In this way, my emotions offer me an opportunity to grow and become intimate with my inner self.

▼

I can own and experience a panicky feeling.

Be happy alchemy of mind.
They turn to pleasure all they find.

Matthew Green

▼

Soul and Mystery

I am one with the divine. I know who I am. I am an extension of life. Life extends through me, it surrounds and flows within and without me. I am one in a million, unique unto myself. Spirit is generous with me because I offer soul a loving and open container through which to operate. I only know what I know—the rest is a mystery. Just because I cannot solve the mystery does not mean that I am not a part of it. I am one with the mystery of the divine. Though I cannot touch it, it touches me. Though I cannot see it, it seeks me. Though I cannot feel it, it feels as me. I will not shrink from what is beyond my comprehension. I will stand firm and steady and be a channel for soul and life and mystery.

▼

I am the mystery.

I myself do nothing. The Holy spirit accomplishes all through me.

William Blake

Unconscious Motivations

If I am doing something that doesn't work, today I will look for possible unconscious motivations. Early wounds need to be brought up to a conscious level where I can see and feel them. Repeating self-destructive behaviors is a futile attempt to correct the original imbalance.

I look for deeper reasons.

What is so striking in Flaubert . . . is his probably unconscious insight that behind what pretends to be freedom lies hidden a deep and very early dependency. It is the dependency of someone who was not permitted to say no because his mother could not bear it, and who therefore refuses all his life to commit himself to his partners in the hope of making up for what was never possible with his mother—namely, to say, "I am your child but you have no right to my whole being and my whole life." Since the seducer is able to assume this attitude toward women only as an adult but not in the early relationship with his mother, his conquests cannot undo his original defeat, and since the pain of early childhood is merely concealed, not cured, by these conquests, the old wounds cannot heal. The repetition compulsion is perpetuated.

Alice Miller

▼

Communal Stories

Stories are important. They are creative containers of personal history and they enrich my knowledge and understanding of the people I come from. Everyone needs roots, a sense of belonging. I can ground within and gain perspective on my personal history through stories that arise out of communities to which I belong.

▼

I honor my communities.

Some say that community is based on blood ties, sometimes dictated by choice, sometimes by necessity. And while this is quite true, the immeasurably stronger gravitational field that holds a group together are their stories . . . the common and simple ones they share with one another. Though these may revolve around crises tamed, tragedy averted, death be not denied, help arriving at the last moment, foolish undertakings, hilarity unbounded and so on the tales people tell one another weave a strong fabric that can warm the coldest emotional or spiritual nights. So the stories that rise up out of the group become, over time, both extremely personal and quite eternal, for they take on a life of their own when told over and over again.

Clarissa Pinkola Estés

▾

The All Soul

Plotinus speaks of the individual soul as indivisible from the All Soul. That is, each of us has encoded into our physical, emotional and spiritual being the same stuff of soul contained within the very heart of God. In fact, we are that heart or that soul—one and the same. There is no moment in life when we are separate from soul, no place to go that is without the presence of soul. Soul is anywhere and everywhere. As I deepen my ability to sit quietly within myself, to be present in the here and now, I deepen my connection with my individualized soul, which is one and the same with the universal soul or the All-Soul. I recognize the wisdom of the ancients as equally applicable today. The soul of the ancestors is my soul also. I am connected to history through spiritual energy.

▾

I trust that I am connected to
divine energy from within.

A road that does not lead to other roads, always has to be retraced, unless the traveller chooses to rust at the end of it.

Tehyi Hsieh

Sensory Knowledge

Today I will allow my senses to awaken and sharpen in their ability to take in this magical world that surrounds me. I will learn with my senses. The opposite, I imagine, will also happen; through my senses I will come to touch, see, feel and smell the life around me that is alive with spirit. I am a sensual being. To denigrate my senses, to ignore or deny them is to block off an important connection with soul. My senses give me a way to *experience* the mystery.

My senses are alive with spirit.

Pestalozzi's first principle was that children should be taught to observe (anschauen). The import of this word, however, did not suggest merely "looking": for him it included observing intently with each sense. Each object should be handled, smelled, tasted, listened to, and looked at from a variety of angles. One should be given the name of a thing only after all its properties that the senses can record have been absorbed. Slowly these sense impressions should be increased to include the many objects in the child's environment.

Joan M. Erickson

211

▼

Body Memories

My body carries memory and knowledge. Understanding and thought are distributed throughout all the cells in my body. Who I am is stored in my physical self. Today when I think positively, I will allow and invite my entire body to carry a positive thought. I will instruct each cell within me to be active, healthy and vibrant. Each time that I feel I am getting low on reserves, I will open all of my body to receiving uplifting light and energy from the universe. I am not a talking head—I am a body, mind and spirit, alive in all of me.

▼

I ask my body to wake up and live.

Those sessions with Ed clarified what I had intuited . . . that matters of the spirit as well as memories, emotions and ideas are embedded in muscle, intestine and lungs. They are not separate things, but layers of the self . . . In the precise moment of feeling his elbow in my gluteal muscles, I could focus on a sharp physical pain, or the memory of my father's anger, or the bliss of merging with cosmic forces. They were all there in that single instant.

Don Hanlon Johnson

Seeing Soul in People

Love comes in many forms—the soul individualizes and expresses itself through people. When I look at those I love today, I will see their souls, their divinity, the God who dwells within them. Soul is both universal and individual. The expression of soul through people is touched by the divine. This is one of the truest and deepest gifts of life.

I see soul in those I love.

When you are old and grey and full of sleep,
And nodding by the fire, take down this book
And slowly read and dream of the soft look
Your eyes had once, and of their shadows deep.

How many loved your moments of glad grace,
And loved your beauty with love false or true,
But one man loved the pilgrim soul in you,
And loved the sorrows of your changing face.
And bending down beside the glowing bars
Murmur, a little sad, from us fled Love.
He paced upon the mountains far above,
And hid his face amid a crowd of stars.

W. B. Yeats

Genuineness

Today I will be genuine. Soul can only function well through a clean and wholesome vehicle. Ultimately, it is my genuineness and my sincerity that will be recognized and rewarded by life. When I am true and sincere, I receive help and support from unseen regions—I open myself up to what is good and pure. Others recognize and reward sincerity. They appreciate it and don't feel compromised or taken advantage of when they lend a helping hand. Living a genuine life aligns my energies with what is good and positive in this world. It opens me to the clean energy of soul and allows more of me to operate. When I am genuine, I am fully who I am. By being this I have access to what makes me unique. When I am unique, I have something to offer that only I can offer, something to give that only I can give.

I am a genuine and sincere person.

God offers to every mind its choice between truth and repose.

Ralph Waldo Emerson

Challenges Along the Path

If I am truly in search of self, I have chosen a difficult path. Looking at my own unconscious will inevitably bring deep anxiety and fear, but I can stay with it. I will not abandon myself at these crucial moments.

Why not ask for more?

One of them (the crisis) is a sudden discouragement about it all. He (the spiritual seeker) wonders whether it is worthwhile. Old doubts and feelings, which he thought were far behind him, suddenly loom up again. He is stabbed by dread that the whole thing may be only a dream world of his own illusions. Such periods of temptation are perfectly normal; expect them to come. . . .
Another crisis is the uneasiness of self-condemnation. There is no one in the entire world who condemns you. You yourself are the only person who condemns you— and pointlessly. In reality, there is no condemnation whatever, but, as long as you think there is, you ache. Not only that, but a man dwelling with the illusion of self-condemnation is compulsively driven to do things that increase the illusion. There is no man, nor god, nor past experience to condemn you. You are free and you are free right now. Will you try to see this?

Vernon Howard

Inner Symbols

My dreams offer me a window into my own internal depths, revealing to me what I dare not know consciously. The symbolic language of my dreams carries with it a sort of congealed meaning, containing both my own personal symbols and the symbols and archetypes of the collective unconscious. By exploring and intuiting the significance of my dreams, I will understand more about how I am affected by and experiencing my life situations.

I study my dreams.

For one thing, dreams are limitless repositories of our deepest emotions. During our waking hours we psychologically censor and dismiss great chunks of what we feel. But the fact that we do not admit our deepest, most intense feelings into consciousness does not mean that the forbidden emotions evaporate or self-destruct. Those feelings that we deny or banish from consciousness go into hiding in our unconscious.
Since dreams are a panoramic window into our unconscious, we find in dreams the emotions that we dared not consciously acknowledge while awake.

J. Allen Hobson

Parenthood

I recognize that what I pass on to my progeny on a person-to-person level is my greatest gift to them. Anyone can give from the excess of their possessions, but a gift of self to another person has more power to sustain than money or things. I can pass pain, alienation and misunderstanding down through the generations, or I can pass a willingness to love and compromise. I can teach my children to live for the beauty and mystery of life or to live for accolades and status. When I share who I really am with my children and grandchildren, I am giving them what no one else can—gifts they can draw strength from for a lifetime. When I withhold from and short-change my children and grandchildren, I am cheating them and their society because they are the culture makers of tomorrow.

What I pass on matters.

Feminism is the most revolutionary idea there has ever been. Equality for women demands a change in the human psyche more profound than anything Marx dreamed of. It means valuing parenthood as much as we value banking.

Polly Toynbee

JULY 18

The Modern Mystic

I become a modern mystic when I know that the source of self-nurturing comes from within. Discipline can be seen as arising out of awareness. Once I am willing to be conscious of the effect of my actions on both myself and those around me, I know that to hurt myself is to hurt another, and to hurt another is to hurt myself. This is how I can use my relationships to perceive the infinite. By allowing myself to feel truly connected to another person, I help to create a sort of dwelling place for the holy spirit. We carve out of the object-worship atmosphere of modern culture, a sacred space where, for a brief time, we contain and invite the presence of soul.

We create a space for soul.

O Lord, the veils of matter conceal Thee from me. How long wilt Thou remain invisible behind the lovely screens of lilies and roses, the clouds of burning gold, and the silent star-decked night? Though they hide Thee, I love them because they hint at Thy presence. Yet I yearn to see Thee as Thou truly art, Thy robes of creation laid aside.

Paramahanse Yogananda

A World of One

I can enter a higher state of consciousness by recognizing the essential oneness of all things. All that is alive issues from the same source. When I tune into this aliveness on a daily level, my mind expands to include more of life, I tune into a higher state of God consciousness, I move closer to the source. By focusing and centering my mind, I can consciously alter my psychic space, I can positively impact the way in which I experience reality and the world that surrounds me.

I am one with the source.

Your growth into higher consciousness can be more rapid if you keep a Catalyst going in your mind as a foreground figure against which all of your sensations, feelings, and thoughts are the background. The Catalyst ALL WAYS US LIVING LOVE can be slowly and silently repeated to enable you to continuously tune in to that part of you that does not see others as him, her, or them—but always us. Oneness is yours when you feel everyone as only us—when you see things through the eyes of others and feel things within their psychic space as though it were your own.

Ken Keyes, Jr.

Admitting Fault

If I look at a problem that I am involved with from all angles, I may come to see that I am partially at fault for a miscommunication or a destructive dynamic. If this happens, I will need to have the strength of character to admit my own fault to myself rather than to blame another. After I get this far, I may see that a change in my behavior is necessary in order to set the situation in a more positive motion; it will improve my side of the dynamic.

I am willing to admit error.

Even if we recognize a conflict as such, we must be willing and able to renounce one of the two contradictory issues. But the capacity for clear and conscious renunciation is rare, because our feelings and beliefs are muddled, and perhaps because in the last analysis most people are not secure and happy enough to renounce anything. Finally, to make a decision presupposes the willingness and capacity to assume responsibility for it. This would include the risk of making a wrong decision and the willingness to bear the consequences without blaming others for them.

Karen Horney, M.D.

Acts of Kindness

Small acts of kindness allow me to touch souls with another person—to reach out over the great divide and brush for a moment the hand and heart of another. An act of kindness is never wasted. It benefits the giver as much or more than the receiver. Anyone who gives with the heart strengthens that muscle within themselves; it is the aerobic training of the spirit. I will not expect soul to just enter my life by chance. I will prepare myself, clean the vehicle that is me, resolve conflicts that tie my mind up and drain my energy. When I am less self-centered, I am able to take the personhood of another into consideration.

I enjoy being kind for kindness' sake.

And this more human love (which will consummate itself infinitely, thoughtfully and gently, and well and clearly in binding and loosing) will be something like that which we are preparing with struggle and toil, the love which consists in the mutual guarding, bordering and saluting of two solitudes.

Rainer Maria Rilke

▼

Contribution

This soul energy is not only a personal one—it is an idea whose time has come, a political force. I will unite myself with like-minded people and refuse to be discouraged. One by one, we will change our society for the better. I will do my part and work toward what is right and good. At the very least, it will make my day feel more purposeful and at the most, I will be doing my little part to make this world a better place—to leave some section of it that I have touched improved rather than diminished for my presence.

▼

I will make a contribution today.

But those who desire to understand, who are looking to find that which is eternal, without beginning and end, will walk together with greater intensity, will be a danger to everything which is unessential, to unrealities, to shadows. And they will concentrate, they will become the flame, because they understand . . . Because of that true friendship . . . there will be real cooperation on the part of each one. And this is not because of authority.

J. Krishnamurti

Working with Love

What I do today, I will do with love in my heart.
The love that I bring to the various tasks and encounters of my day weave that energy into the very fabric of my world. This world is sewn invisibly together with waves and particles. The waves and particles emanating from me move in and out of a similar field of those surrounding another person. The energy I send is felt by another person on a deeper level than anything I might say. It doesn't work to be polite with my words but then to feel hate—people get a double message. Double messages make people feel crazy and teach those close to me to doubt their own insides.

I will work with love.

And what is it to work with love?
It is to weave the cloth with threads drawn from your heart,
even as if your beloved were to wear that cloth.
It is to build a house with affection,
even as if your beloved were to dwell in that house. . . .
It is to charge all things you fashion with
a breath of your own spirit.

Kahlil Gibran

▼

Inner Depth

I believe in life today and I am not afraid to admit it. I know what is eternally good in this universe because I experience it daily. Within my own heart there is a well of love that I constantly turn to; within my own soul there is a faith in the universe, in life, that never leaves me. Occasionally I leave it, but it is always there when I return, right where I left it, in the stillness of my own being. For me to have faith feels natural. I sense that I am alive and I see the life that surrounds me. I trust the fundamental goodness of this universe. I know, in my heart, that with sincere effort, adversity can be overcome and good will win out over evil. In any case, I know that I can allow the best of me to conquer the worst of me—that I can constantly reach toward my higher self.

▼

I believe in life.

A deep man believes that the evil eye can wither,
that the heart's blessing can heal
and that love can overcome all odds.

Ralph Waldo Emerson

Genuine Health

Today I do not see a life free of problems as a healthy life. Wanting my life to look and to be problem-free goes against what is natural and mobilizes my vanity in the struggle to hide anything that I consider "unpleasant." Problems that I hide don't go away. It is facing adversity and pain in the light of day, sharing it with others—breaking isolation and connecting with those around me—that promotes growth. When I want my day to be struggle-free, I stop the wheels of life from functioning. Problems are a part of living well and being alive.

If I have life, I will have problems.

The point that health is not so much the absence *of disease as it is the* presence *of an optimal healing process is crucial for understanding our lives. It is crucial because the principle applies not only to our physical health but also to our mental health and to the health of our organizations and institutions. A healthy organization—whether a marriage, a family, or a business corporation—is not one with an absence of problems, but one that is actively and effectively addressing or healing its problems.*

M. Scott Peck, M.D.

225

▼

One Step

I will take a small step toward positive change today. All I need do is improve some aspect of my life for one day, today. Rather than letting a bothersome situation fester and get worse or just stay the same, I will make a move to improve it. There is no reason why I can't get my life, body, health, work, recreation or relationships into a better place. If I am not happy with the way something is going for me, then today is the day to try something different. When I am willing to take a small risk or make a forward move, I am justified in asking for help from the universe—I am doing my part.

▼

I will take one step.

We have problems here of much smoking and alcoholism. Some of these problems are things we can tackle by impressing on people the need to look after themselves better. . . . I honestly don't think the problem has anything to do with poverty. . . . The problem very often for people is, I think, just ignorance and failing to realize that they do have some control over their lives.

Edwina Currie

Loving Another

When I love someone or when someone loves me, we become a part of one another. To the extent to which that love carries commitment along with it, we are partners in each other's destiny. What we do affects the other, a piece of us lives in the heart and mind of that other person. What piece of me do I want to live on in the mind of another? When they turn inward to find me, who will they find? What will I have left behind me as a legacy of that relationship? I may have made mistakes or hurt someone without understanding what I was doing, but today I will be mindful; I'll keep myself honest and try not to harm. I cannot control how another person acts or feels, but I can be aware of what I put into a relationship.

I have conscious interactions.

Love is the extra effort we make in our dealings with those whom we do not like and once you understand that, you understand all. This idea that love overtakes you is nonsense. This is but a polite manifestation of sex. To love another you have to undertake some fragment of their destiny.

Quentin Crisp

God in Nature

Those who have been able to tune into and appreciate nature have had the ability to see God behind the illusion of reality. Though this world feels to me as if it is still and concrete, the truth is that it is always in motion. The world is in a constant state of birth and death, manifestation and destruction. Today as I walk through my day, I will look at the world through soft eyes, eyes that see not only at but through. As an exercise in raising my consciousness, I will remind myself throughout my day to tune into a world in motion. I will attempt to see the hand of creation behind all that surrounds me. When I look at the world, I will take a deep breath, quiet my mind and know that I am looking at the many manifestations of soul.

The world is God and soul made manifest.

The perfumed flowers are our sisters . . .
the juices of the meadows,
all body heat of the pony, and man—
all belong to the same family.

Chief Seattle

228

▼

Taking vs. Receiving

There is a vast difference between taking and receiving. There is a way of receiving that is also giving. When I can receive, I act as a willing container for another person's gift. I validate the giver's act of giving and acknowledge his or her generosity. This benefits both the giver and the receiver in equal measure, both are enriched and neither overly depleted.

When I take, I do not acknowledge the gift—rather, I put in the purse of my being that which I want, then snap it shut and go off to take again, hoping that no one notices. This leaves both parties wanting—the giver feels she has been manipulated into giving whether wanting to or not; and the taker—because without *receiving* a person never really fills up—just continues to feel empty.

▼

I can acknowledge a gift; I can receive.

Developing the muscles of the soul demands no competitive spirit, no killer instinct, although it may erect pain barriers that the spiritual athlete must crash through.

Germaine Greer

Honesty

Keeping secrets is a foolish attempt to stay safe from the truth. We tell ourselves we are sparing another person or protecting ourselves, but all too often the secrets that we keep actually keep us. What people need from me in order to make sense of me is the truth. When I withhold that truth, I withhold myself. I am creating distance that no one can cross because the way across the divide is the way of honesty. I cannot make something better by lying, and I cannot be fully understood if I won't give the benefit of the truth. I can live my life in a web of lies without ever uttering a falsehood. The web of lies is composed of not just what I say, but the vast amount of honesty that I withhold.

There is a difference between considerate honesty and aggressive frankness. Honesty recognizes the personhood of both people and is an act of trust; but too much frankness can border on mean.

▼

I see honesty as an act of trust.

The weakness of a soul is proportionate to the number of truths that must be kept from it.

Eric Hoffer

▼

Being Useful

I will make my life useful and relevant today. I am not an alien living in isolation from planet earth. I am a part of the world I live in and there are countless ways for me to participate in co-creating this society. When I do what I see needs to be done, I am working in accord with the natural evolution of society, with what needs to happen, and I will have support from unexpected corners. Because I am addressing a need rather than imposing my needs and desires, I am flowing with the tide instead of against it.

Spirit moves in invisible ways. This world is made of and designed by spirit energy. When I work with the needs of the universe, I work with spirit. I co-create this world. Spirit and matter issue from the one particle. When I am in touch with and being useful to this world, I am in line with divine energy.

▼

I co-create the world.

I look for what needs to be done . . . After all, that's how the universe designs itself.

Buckminister Fuller

August

Though I speak with the tongues of men and of
angels, and have not love, I am become as
sounding brass, or a tinkling cymbal.

And though I have the gift of prophecy, and
understand all mysteries, and all knowledge;
and though I have faith, so that I could
remove mountains, and have not love, I am
nothing.

And though I bestow all my goods to feed the
poor and though I give my body to be
burned, and have not love, it profiteth me
nothing.

Love suffereth long, and is kind; love envieth not; love vaunteth not itself, is not puffed up,

Doth not behave itself unseemly, seeketh not her own, is not easily provoked, thinketh no evil;

Rejoiceth not in iniquity, but rejoiceth in the truth;

Beareth all things, believeth all things, hopeth all things, endureth all things.

Love never faileth: but whether there be prophecies, they shall fail; whether there be tongues, they shall cease; whether there be knowledge, it shall vanish away.

For we know in part, and we prophesy in part.

But when that which is perfect is come, then that which is in part shall be done away.

When I was a child, I spake as a child, I understood as a child, I thought as a child: but when I became a man, I put away childish things.

For now we see through a glass, darkly; but then face to face: now I know in part; but then shall I know even as also I am known.

And now abideth faith, hope, love, these three; but the greatest of these is love.

Paul's letter to the Corinthians 13:1-13

Seeing Innocence

I will take a different view of a person today. When I resent people, I tend to see only their faults. I am seeing what it is that annoys me about them and, in a sense, withholding my good opinion. An attitude like this can doom an encounter with them to failure. What I say and see on the nonverbal level through my attitude, body language and the feeling I put into the atmosphere is very powerful. When I see people in this black and white fashion, I am not seeing them.

I will see another person's innocence.

It is suggested that we begin the encounter with an entirely different kind of mind set. We resolve beforehand that we will scan the other person for signs of love, gentleness and peace, and that the only information we will retain in our mind is that which will permit us to continue looking upon this person kindly. In other words, we seek only their innocence, not their guilt. We look at them with our heart, not with our preconceived notions. This approach is one we all can use in our daily lives . . . whether at work or in our more intimate relationships.

Gerald G. Jampoksky, M.D.

Working with Trouble

I will not shrink from trouble and tell myself that it is not of God. I will not divide the spirit and the flesh and cast half of me into darkness. Spirit and flesh issue from the same source. When I cut myself in half like this, I am a stranger in both worlds; I belong nowhere. I was designed to engage in all of life, to move through the trials of the world and know that they too are part of building the human spirit—part of the mind and heart of God.

▼

I use problems as stepping stones.

God the helpful, strong and benignant preserver is also God the devourer and destroyer. The torment of the couch of pain and evil on which we are racked is his touch as much as happiness and sweetness and pleasure. It is only when we see with the eye of the complete union and feel this truth in the depths of our being that we can entirely discover behind that mask too the calm and beautiful face of the all-blissful Godhead and in this touch that tests our imperfection the touch of the friend and builder of the spirit in man.

Sri Aurobindo

▼

Dying to the Vehicle

Today I dis-identify with my body and identify with that which is timeless, infinite and eternal. My body is the vehicle through which the spirit is made flesh. All of my body is contained within my mind, but all of my mind is not contained within my body. I am more than mere flesh—I am light and divine energy, a piece of eternity. When I know that I am more than my body, that my body is the vehicle through which soul is made manifest, then I can become a channel of transcendent, divine, God energy.

I am eternity, which is beyond
body and mind.

This is an essential experience of any mystical revelation. . . . you identify yourself with the consciousness and life of which your body is but the vehicle you die to the vehicle and identify yourself with the consciousness of that of which the vehicle is only the carrier . . . identify behind the surface display of duality—all of these are manifestations of the one—the one shines through all things. This is the realization of God.

Joseph Campbell

Having a Mission

Today I will recognize the connection between mental health and a mission in life. When I carry a positive mission in my mind and heart that I wish to accomplish in this world, I mobilize unseen forces, the world moves in and helps. I give my soul an opportunity to deepen and grow; I energize it when I give it specific tasks to accomplish. This world moves forward through the acts of humankind. It is people who evolve and co-evolve with society. We are co-creators of this world in which we live. If I am truly intelligent and have good ideas to offer, then let me offer them. Who cares if they are received just perfectly—if they are worthwhile they will find their way, unseen hands will guide them toward their proper target. I will have faith, I will have soul, I will have a meaningful mission.

I have a mission in my life.

Find a mission in life and take it seriously.

Dr. William C. Menninger

Interaction

There is no such thing in quantum physics as the passive observer. Whether the observer is aware of it or not, physical events are affected by the mere presence of another person. The simple act of observation actually alters the result of a physical experiment. The truth is that even if what I am looking at seems to be still and separate from me, I still affect it. My thoughts and the events of the world are connected. When I have a thought, it enters the world of probabilities and affects an outcome. Both my thoughts and this world are alive. They interact to co-create my day-to-day reality.

My world and I are interconnected.

The "I" arises from the brain through a particular quantum physical mechanism called quantum correlation . . . because quantum physical events may be occurring in neural tissue. . . . The mind enters the body in such events by altering these probabilities in much the same way that an observer alters the probabilities of events by observing them.

Fred Alan Wolf, Ph.D.

Simple Things

Today I will learn to see soul in the simple things of life. It is oftentimes the things that I take for granted that are truly responsible for the deep under-pinnings of my sense of well being and personal happiness. When I let myself *have* and *enjoy* events of life, I will see soul radiate from the simple and the little things. Life is a tapestry woven of small threads.

I appreciate what I take for granted.

I walked through hospital corridors, going into rooms, asking people who had things I was afraid of. "Why do you want to live? How do you manage?" . . . What impressed me was that the lists did not contain pages of philosophical discussion about the meaning of life. They said things that were so simple. "I painted a picture," said someone with no fingers: a brush had to be tied to her hand. "I looked out the window, and it is a beautiful day." "The nurse rubbed my back." "My family called and are coming to see me." The lists just went on with simple daily events. And I began to realize that this is really what life is about.

Bernie S. Siegel, M.D.

▼

A Sense of Purpose

I will use the circumstances that life offers in order to strengthen my will and become a dynamic, effective person. I will center myself and focus in on a direction and purpose for my life. When I understand my own direction, I will move toward it in all ways that are available to me. Even the smallest thing is worth doing.

▼

I will take a small action.

I have just mentioned three important ways to make your will dynamic: (1) choose a simple task or an accomplishment that you have never mastered and determine to succeed with it; (2) be sure you have chosen something constructive and feasible, then refuse to consider failure; (3) concentrate on a single purpose, using all abilities and opportunities to forward it. But you should always be sure, within the calm region of your inner Self, that what you want is right for you to have, and in accord with life's purposes. You can then use all the force of your will to accomplish your object; keep your mind, however, centered on the thought of God—the Source of all power and all accomplishment.

Paramahansa Yogananda

Being Alive

Let me be real. Let me take risks and feel alive. Numbness is the opposite of life, a slow, imperceptible death of the soul. What I have and who I am, I will feel. If it is sad, I won't run from that emotion. Better to hurt and be alive than to be numb and walk through life marking time. If I love I will lose and if I lose I will hurt, but I will love again. Feelings and experiences are cyclical like the seasons. I will dress for the weather by asking God to be with me so that I can be a living, breathing part of this world.

▼

I will hold my space.

Death is Not Evil, Evil is Mechanical

Only the human being, absolved from kissing and strife
goes on and on and on, without wandering
fixed upon the jib of the ego
going, yet never wandering, fixed, yet in motion,
the kind of hell that is real, grey and awful
sinless and stainless going round and round
the kind of hell grey Dante never saw
but of which he had a bit inside him

D. H. Lawrence

Stepping Back

Keeping a broad view in mind allows me to keep my sense of perspective—it keeps me from getting lost in unimportant details. In order to do this I will practice an attitude of some detachment. I will step back from my thought process just to see how my day feels when I act as a witness to my mental process. I will be a watcher of my own process of thinking, an observer within my own mind. I can better grasp the larger picture when I do not get derailed in obsessive mental machinations. I feel better about my life and it makes more sense to me when I accept that it has an overall purpose and plan. I will relax, let go and enjoy the ride.

I will take a deep breath and step back.

A tourist visiting Italy came upon the construction site of a huge church. "What are you doing?" he asked three stonemasons who were working at their trade.

"I'm cutting stone," answered the first tersely.

"I'm cutting stone for twenty lire a day," the second responded.

"I'm helping build a great cathedral," the third stonemason announced.

from *And I Quote*

Things of the World

I will not chase after shadows today. I will not ask the things of the world to fill my soul. Any experience, object or passion cannot make up for, eliminate or otherwise fill up a hole within me. When I ask the world to complete my insides, I am asking it for more than it can offer. The world is limited in what it can give me. Bitter though this awareness may be, it is my road to truly enjoying the world as it is. When I learn the true value of worldly gains, what the things of the world can and cannot offer, I cease asking them to be what they cannot. People, places and things cannot *make* me happy. I have to do that for myself. It is my ability to use and enjoy objects, rather than letting objects own me, that gives my life its pleasant rhythm.

I value things correctly.

Every real object must cease to be what it seemed, and none could ever be what the whole soul desired.

George Santayana

Simple Pleasures

I have simple tastes, I am easy to please. Today I will not pound my fist on the table of life demanding more from it than I am willing to give to it. When I can take pleasure in ordinary things and joy from everyday experience, life fills me, feels satisfying. This attitude allows me to use what I have. I recognize that it is not what I have but how I value and enjoy it that generates happiness.

I am happy.

Blest, who can unconcern'dly find
Hours, days, and years slide soft away
In health of body, peace of mind;
Quiet by day,
Sound sleep by night; study and ease
Together mixed; sweet recreation;
And innocence, which most does please
     with meditation.
Thus let me live, unseen, unknown;
Thus unlamented let me die;
Steal from the world, and not a stone
Tell where I lie.

Alexander Pope

▼

Letting Go of Faults

If there is something about myself that I don't like, I can let it go. My attachment to a negative quality in me can create a strong sort of hidden shame. When I can release it, I create a sort of vacuum that the universe quickly, even instantaneously moves in to fill. The vacuum I create by releasing rigid and dysfunctional thought patterns creates a kind of inner space—it allows room for something new to rush in. When I can elevate my level of vibration in this way, I grow. Negative thoughts and feelings are dense, and I can feel almost glued in place by them. They begin to have a life of their own, and that life is powerful within me. Consciously releasing them, letting them rise up and out of my inner world into space, even in what may feel like an unfinished state, can allow me to see and experience them and myself differently. It can open up new psychic space and let me live from a higher place inside of myself.

▼

I am elevating my level of living.

When you have faults do not fear to abandon them.

Confucius

▼

Commonality

I acknowledge the humanity in other people. Who I am, they are also. I need not fear exposure because all the secrets that I think I keep so well hidden from others are only too visible, only too obvious. I am more transparent than I think, but I am not alone—others are transparent, too. We are all insecure. We all feel love, hate and fear rejection. We are maddeningly alike under the skin. If I am to be unusual and unique, it will not be so much because I try to be different, but because at a deep and spiritual level, I recognize the essential sameness of all people. I can live with the understanding that human beings are fundamentally similar.

▼

I see divine spirit in all people.

Learn to see God in all persons, of whatever race or creed. You will know what divine love is when you begin to feel your oneness with every human being, not before. In mutual service we forget the little self and glimpse the one measureless self, the spirit that unifies all men.

Parmahansa Yogananada

Appreciation

Today I am grateful just for this day. Being alive is a gift, a gift that I will not take for granted. I am a lucky person. I am blessed and have the wisdom to count my blessings. When I take stock of all that I have to appreciate, I am actually creating abundance in my life. The act of appreciating allows good to maintain its presence in my day. When I see and expect good, I recognize it when it comes, I alter my self concept, I program myself for positive experiences to enter my life. This kind of awareness comes from a wise and an open place within me. It shows life that I recognize its good intentions. It aligns me with energies that are positive—those that manifest beauty and well being.

I appreciate and expect good in my day.

Man is fond of counting his troubles, but he does not count his joys. If he counted them up as he ought to, he would see that every lot has enough happiness provided for it.

Feodor Dostoyevsky

Going Within

Going within can be terrifying; to be willing to truly be still and with my self is not easy. Because it can be such a despairing feeling to go within and not find what I need, rather than tolerate the emptiness I race head-long into the acquisition of more of what I think will fill me. When I live suspended amidst the promise of fulfillment, I see the solution to emptiness as adding and subtracting outside experiences. Each time I leave a job or a relationship, the parts of myself that I left unre-solved are still within me. Until I resolve them, all I am doing is creating more complication in my life. This keeps me busy with the illusion that I am working on my problem, which only too often is not the problem at all. The problem is generally within myself. Until I am willing to look for it there, all the switching and chang-ing in the world won't give me what I need.

▼

I have the strength to be still.

You are so afraid of losing your moral sense that you are not willing to take it through anything more dangerous than a mud-puddle.

Gertrude Stein

Alone in the Presence of the Self

When I do not allow myself the time to develop an inner relationship with my own soul, I leave myself open to countless maladies. I am alone in the presence of myself. Being alone in the presence of self is the worst kind of aloneness. There is something very disturbing about not being able to be comfortable with my own insides. The reason that a process of introspection is so vital on the road toward self is just this: when I sit quietly with myself, all the unfinished business, old hurts and unquenched longings begin to rumble around and make themselves felt to me. If I cannot sit through this process of feeling my painful feelings, sorting through them and resolving them, I really cannot sit with myself because sitting with myself is too painful. When I have sorted out the problem and learned methods of sitting with inner pain, I am able to sit through these feelings so that I can eventually get to serenity and self.

I am willing to sit with all of who I am.

Neurosis is the way of avoiding non-being by avoiding being.

Paul Tillich

▼

The Dream of Perfection

One of the surest paths toward feelings of inadequacy and an inability to move forward in life is to set unrealistic goals for myself. That is, to have standards that represent "getting there" that are so high that I always fall short. More likely, the effect of these overly high standards will be to keep me from ever beginning because the point of arrival looks too far away, and I cannot imagine how to find and take all of the intermediate steps.

Today I will be realistic. I know that there is no such thing as perfect, so why should I worry about getting there? *There* is the here and now, and when I get *there*, it will be that day's here and now. I recognize that perfection is only an illusion, and I will learn to take daily pleasure and fulfillment from the process.

▼

I live in today.

We have trained them (men) to think of the Future as a promised land which favored heroes attain—not as something which everyone reaches at the rate of sixty minutes an hour, whatever he does, whoever he is.

C. S. Lewis

▼

The Highest Energy

Rather than wait for a second coming, I will recognize the presence of Christ, God or the Prophets within me. I have available to me an inner vision through which I can access soul. When I sit quietly and turn inward, my own soul and the soul of the world presents itself to me. It rolls before me, it rises from within; it fills me with peace and tranquility. Rather than wait for someone to tell me where soul is, I will allow soul itself to show me where it lives. When I recognize this energy within myself, I am also able to see it around me. Soul is not complicated—it is simple. When I live with soul, I live in line with my best self.

▼

I recognize the highest energy.

Paul asked: What was there about the human condition that made Jesus necessary? He answered, particularly in the letter to the Romans, by saying that it was the total inability of people to realize their own best intentions . . . God, therefore, acted in Christ (according to Paul) to transform the whole situation and to restore to men a direct inspiration of life and conduct.

Phil Cousineau

An Alive Universe

Seeing the universe as alive in the present moment alters my sense of life. What goes around comes around. What gets missed in one day will re-present itself in another form. The frantic rush to accumulate experience in order to fill me leaves me feeling emptier than before. If the experiencer is not engaged on equal terms with the experience, then energy does not get exchanged and I do not fill up. The soul experience allows me to trust life because trust is an implicit part of this exchange of energy. Part of trust is the feeling of being held, of not being dropped. The soul experience allows me to be held by life. Eventually I come to the understanding that if I drop, I will only drop into more of life or more of the soul experience of living.

There is only life.

Can anxious thought add one day to our lives? Consider the lilies of the field, they do not sow, nor do they reap, but I say unto you that even Solomon in all his glory was not arrayed as one of these.

Matthew 6:28-29

I Am Light

I am a child of the universe, fundamentally good. If you dig deep within me, you will find something beautiful and real; you will find spirit. I am not afraid of the light within me and I feel no need to bury it today. Rather than hide my own inner light, I will let it shine through me. When I walk through my day, I will let this light be in me, widen and increase; I will let it look upon others. It is a beautiful thing to have a light within me. I radiate, I shimmer, I glow. I am the vehicle through which soul becomes an actualized force. Today I accept that soul works through me.

▼

I am fundamentally good.

Do all the good you can,
By all the means you can,
In all the ways you can,
In all the places you can,
At all the times you can,
To all the people you can,
As long as ever you can.

John Wesley's *Role*

▼

Getting Even

I come to points on my path toward soulfulness when I am faced with letting go of old resentment and hurt. One of the major blocks to moving beyond this pain is my desire for retribution. I want to make the person who hurt me suffer as I feel they made me suffer. Unfortunately, though, the hatred and resentment that I carry in my heart for another person is carried exactly there—in *my* heart. If I could truly place it on the other person without having to carry it within me, my retribution would be complete. But in getting back at them I also am getting back at myself; I am twice hurt, initially when they hurt me and now by carrying anger and rage for them within my very being. They continue in this way to have tremendous power over me.

I realize today that I am more powerful than my own resentment and more important than my wish to hurt. Just for today, I will *act as if* I let go of an old pain.

▼

I let go.

The discovery of what is true and the practice of that which is good are the two most important objects of philosophy.

Voltaire

▼

A Life Well Lived

There is no substitute for a life well lived. Soul cannot be felt or expressed through a life that is in shambles. The kind of inner security and continuity that a carefully lived life offers is its own reward. No therapy or philosophy can really be effective unless I live a life that is clean and wholesome. If I think I can conduct myself in a dubious manner and get good and happy results, I am misunderstanding the laws of living. I will reap what I sow. If I sow seeds of disharmony and discontent, if I live a life that lacks commitment and follow-through, then that is the experience I am creating for myself. If I live a life that is not loving and well-intended, there is no way that I will reap those rewards. Whatever it is I wish to receive, I need to first create and live in my own life.

▼

I put clean and wholesome living
as my highest priority.

*There is only one thing that is fully our own and that
is our will or purpose.*

Epictetus, 1st century A.D.

Setting a Positive Goal

I will set a positive goal for myself today and take one small step toward achieving it. Setting positive goals for one's life and experiencing them as already happening helps to clear negativity and open channels for positive, soulful living. This is nothing more than living with a clear awareness that there is a reality beyond the scene or the objects that surround me. Though my spiritual path leads me to be increasingly comfortable with going within myself, I still remain an alive and active participant in the world. Learning to set the kinds of goals that actualize aspects of the self is living in line with soul. Soul is life-giving, constantly engaged in the act of creation, in the miracle of coming forth.

I am able to set a goal and follow through.

Ah, but a man's reach should exceed his grasp,
Or What's a heaven for?

Robert Browning

Seizing the Moment

I will not hold back today. I will seize the moment. All the excitement and beauty of life is just as present in it as is or ever will be possible. There is nowhere else to be. This is it. The potential for life is here and now; there is not nor could there be another, more important or soul-filled moment.

I will eat the fruit.

This is just to say
I have eaten
the plums
that were in
the icebox

and which
you were probably
saving
for breakfast

Forgive me
they were delicious
so sweet
and so cold

William Carlos Williams

Pointing the Way

I will live the life I have. All the lessons that I need to learn are spiritually present within the situations of my day. Life and spirit are one. A block in my life can be seen as a block in my spirit. When I use the circumstances of my life as grist for the mill of self-knowledge, when I see working with my own inner pain and suffering as my personal path toward soul, then and only then, my life becomes transcendent. It is that awareness that allows me to die to the flesh and be reborn to the spirit. Then I can use my life to serve a higher purpose. The life I have been given is my path toward soul. It is meant to contain my search, my struggle toward self. It can set me free. Through learning to understand the mystery behind daily events, I can go from blindness to seeing. I will use the life I have been given to guide me toward soul.

I say yes to suffering.

The man pulling radishes
pointed the way
with a radish.

Issa

Only Soul

There is only soul. Only one reality, one truth. When I tune into the deeper layers of life, the world appears to be a stage set. As I move through my day, I will look beyond and beneath the surface. I will slow down and allow time and space to expand in my presence. Time and space actually alter the way that they feel to me when I am quiet and contemplative; their very qualities seem different when I move further into the moment, experiencing it more deeply. Life takes on a richness and a fullness that has nothing to do with anything more than just being. Just being, fully in this moment, allows its beauty to slowly unfold itself before me—to spread its wealth at my feet. Living here and now is enough.

I allow the richness of the moment
to alter time and space.

Before the revelations of the soul, Time and Space and Nature shrink away.

Ralph Waldo Emerson

Unconscious Anger

The kind of anger that I use as a hiding place is largely unconscious. Acting it out is simply another way to keep it unconscious or to not feel it. When I get triggered, I blame someone else; I see the other as responsible for my bitterness. My unconscious is saying, "You are of great significance because I depend upon you for my happiness, for my position or prestige. Through you I fulfill, so you are important to me; I must guard you, I must possess you. Through you I escape from myself; and when I am thrown back upon myself, being fearful of my own state, I become angry." Anger takes many forms—disappointment, resentment, bitterness, jealousy. When I project it mindlessly onto someone else, making it about them rather than me, I disown a piece of myself and I lose my potential to learn about how I really feel.

I am able to own my own anger.

We condemn others and that very condemnation is a justification of ourselves. Without some kind of attitude whether self righteous or self abasement, what are we?

Chogyan Trungpa

A Tortuous Path of Soul Loss

If I sincerely choose a spiritual path, I will be able to learn to spin straw into gold, to use my inner pain and anguish to burn through to soul. When I feel lost to myself, I will see it as a symptom that I need my care and attention. I will become kinder and take better care of myself so that I can again feel found and seen. It is part of the human condition that I can become alienated from soul.

Alienation is a symptom of soul loss.

What shamans traditionally called soul loss we now think of as emptiness, alienation, or pain. . . . There is a hole where once was soul. The crisis seizes us when we're in the steely grip of grief, betrayal, physical terror, numbing routine, or an unauthentic life. . . . How is it that for the soul to be truly moved . . . a "tortured psychology" may be necessary? That there is an "unfathomable longing in the soul to vex itself," as Edgar Allan Poe darkly described it? That the first step may be to lose the way? To lose our soul so that we may regain it? . . . Though the ferocious reality of soul crisis may often be sanitized today with clinical nomenclature, the ancients said it best: People can and do lose their souls.

Phil Cousineau

Life's Meaning

What I endeavor to do with my day, what I can conjure up in my inner vision, how I perceive the world in which I live: these are what give my life its unique meaning. The meaning in my life is the meaning it has *to me*. Life does not necessarily have intrinsic and specific meaning. I am the experiencer, the filter through which life passes. I create my own personal meaning. I interpret my own experience. I write and edit the contents and impressions of my own day. My personal meaning lies in my own journalistic slant, my intimate interview with life.

I am the creator of my personal meaning.

Calderón said: "All life is a dream, and dreams themselves are only dreams." Ever since man existed he has sought life's meaning. Who are we? Why do we live? What is our goal? Has man been made in the image of God or God in the image of man? Each concept has its opposite; life/death, yes/no, light/shadow. Life's meaning rests in the eye of the beholder and in our constant desire to approach perfection.

Marcel Marceau

▼

Awareness of Death

I welcome an awareness of death into my daily life. I allow it to give shape, depth and meaning to the world around me, to inform my spirit as to the temporary nature of worldly life. Rather than push away the thought of my life ending in fear of that knowledge, I consciously entertain it and let it alter the quality of my day.

▼

Death can walk with me.

This awareness of death is the source of zest for life and of our impulse to create not only works of art, but civilizations as well. Not only is human anxiety universally associated with ultimate death, but awareness of death also brings benefits. . . . the more aware we are of death, the more vividly we experience the fact that it is not only beneath our dignity to tell a lie but useless as well. Rome will not burn a second time, so why fiddle during this burning? We can then say with Omar, "The Bird of Time has but a little way to flutter—and the Bird is on the Wing." The men of wisdom throughout history have understood the value for life in our awareness of death. "To philosophize," said Cicero, "is to prepare for death." And Seneca stated, "No man enjoys the true taste of life but he who is willing and ready to quit it."

Rollo May

Elevation

I will reach above and beyond myself today. I will move upward into my spirit nature. Why should I wait for life to happen to me, for some other person to take responsibility for making my life what it can and should be? I am the person to whom my life has been given. Just as parents are given children to nurture and help grow, I have been given my own life. I will give birth to me, I will care for myself and lead myself toward good things. I will treat my own life with the love and sweet attention that I would give to my own child. In this sense, I am my own child and my own parent. If I don't take care of me who will—who can? I am the only one who's with me 24 hours a day. I know me, I am my own best companion. I will attend to my needs with care and devotion. Listen to my pains and my dreams. I will guide myself responsibly and lovingly toward what will help me to grow and change in positive ways.

I am willing to grow with me.

Make no more giants, God!
But elevate the human race at once!

Robert Browning

September

Student, do the simple purification.
You know that the seed is inside the horse-
    chestnut tree;
and inside the seed there are the blossoms
    of the tree, and the chestnuts, and the
    shade.
So inside the human body there is the seed,
    and inside the seed there is the human
    body again.

Fire, air, earth, water, and space— if you
   don't want the secret one, you can't
   have these either.

Thinkers, listen, tell me what you know of
   that is not inside the soul?
Take a pitcher full of water and set it down
   on the water—now it has water inside
   and water outside
We mustn't give it a name lest silly people
   start talking again about the body and
   the soul.

If you want the truth, I'll tell you the truth:
Listen to the secret sound, the real sound,
   which is inside you.
The one no one talks of speaks the secret
   sound to himself, and he is the one who
   has made it all.

                                             Kabir

▼

Optimism

I will dare to see myself in a positive light today. What do I have to lose? Surely soul wishes me to feel good about myself and to enjoy this abundant world of spirit and mystery. I will be optimistic both about my life and in small encounters throughout my day. When I am negative, I notice those aspects that reinforce my negative self image and, believing myself to be a failure, put less energy into trying to succeed. Conversely, when I am optimistic about my potential, I feel better about my successes and am less put off by failure. This is the basic principle behind the many techniques of positive thinking. The unconscious mental set acts as a form of pre-programming. Throughout daily activity, a person again starts noticing those factors that support his or her mental set, be it positive or negative, and accordingly the opportunities for realizing it.

▼

I will be positive about myself.

What other dungeon is so dark as one's own heart!
What jailer is as inexorable as one's self!

Nathaniel Hawthorne

The Comfort of Ritual

It is often the elders among us who understand the value of rituals and who help to anchor them. Older people who understand how to be elders, who are able to pass on encouragement and strength rather than despair and judgment, are gifts to society. Elders who have worked through their own failures and inadequacies and come to terms with their lives are able to mentor without controlling, give advice without criticizing, and help people who are younger to get in touch with their own strength, their own soul. They provide encouragement to go on with life and to face our challenges with love and courage. Generations are connected to one another seamlessly, each leading naturally into the next. The old receive the vitality of youth, the youth the stability of the old . . . and those in the middle are supported and nurtured in their life's duties.

I accept the teachings of the wise elders.

The hand of liberality is stronger than the arm of power.

Sadi

Quiet Desperation

Today I will not hide pieces and corners of myself from my inner view. When I fail to live up to an image of what I think I should be, I hide who I fear I am. Spirit cannot live a lie. I lie to myself when I pretend not to be who I am, and the person I lie to the most is me. When I do not tell the truth to myself, I undermine my connection with self. I weaken my most important link—me with my own insides, my intellect with my heart. Soul comes to me through my own inner depths. When my inner depths are littered with unopened boxes or rejected pieces of self, it barricades the smooth entry of soul.

I will know myself.

The mass of men lead lives of quiet desperation. What is called resignation is confirmed desperation. . . . A stereotyped but unconscious despair is concealed even under what are called the games and amusements of mankind. There is no play in them, for this comes after work. But it is a characteristic of wisdom not to do desperate things.

Henry David Thoreau

Future Shock

I am a survivor of future shock. I have lived through a period of profound, disorienting social, political and worldwide change. My life has moved quickly, so quickly that my head sometimes spins and I feel lost. Today, rather than get lost in being lost, I will use my day to begin to be found. The journey before me has not been traveled as yet. There are paths open to me that have never been opened up before in history. This territory is raw. It is uncharted, it is wide open to a journey of the mind and the soul. Where others explored and mapped out the territories of land, it is the task of my era to explore and map out the territories of the mind and spirit. The world I find myself living in is concrete and natural, but it also contains the manifestations of the human imagination.

I am an explorer.

Without an organizing center, post modern man is lost, wandering in a wilderness of confusing plurality but, paradoxically, being bereft of set moral landmarks, he is in a unique position to undertake a new journey.

Sam Keen

The Mystical Experience

When I transcend my day-to-day world and connect with a force and truth beyond what my eyes see, I sense that I live in a universe with a higher intelligence, that there is a reality that connects us all, beyond words, shape or form. I have glimpsed eternity and it has changed my life. It has allowed me to go through my life knowing that I am not alone, that life is not meaningless.

I experience the deeper meaning of life.

A mystical experience is . . . usually profound and almost always positive in nature, leading people to move in an ethical direction, leading them to be more confident, to feel that there is meaning in life; leading them to fear death less, making them take a more healthy approach to life in general. These are experiences that are sometimes related to nature, music, and feelings that there have been meaningful coincidences in the person's life, that how could these things have happened except for an antichance power. Sometimes they are conversion experiences and these can be of a gradual nature or a sudden nature.

George Gallup —*from Gallup polls on 4 out of 10 Americans who reported having a mystical experience*

▼

Honest Living

Soul cannot shine through a distorted lens; it cannot operate through a dishonest life, a life filled with pretense and subtle lies. I will be honest and genuine in the way I live. I won't pretend to be what I am not in order to look good. Living well requires a constant vigilance, constant awareness. When I don't pay attention to the way I live, it is all too easy to slip into bad habits and nonproductive ways of thinking, behaving and conducting myself. I will live mindfully today.

▼

I live an honest life.

If you can keep your head when all about you
Are losing theirs and blaming it on you;
If you can trust yourself when all men doubt you,
But make allowance for their doubting, too,
If you can wait and not be tired by waiting,
Or being lied about, don't deal in lies,
Or being hated, don't give way to hating,
And yet don't look too good, nor talk too wise;
If you can dream—and not makes dreams your master,
If you can think—and not make thoughts your aim,
If you can meet Triumph and Disaster
And treat those two impostors just the same.

Rudyard Kipling

Home

I will look for and create places in my life where I feel seen and understood for who I am. Craziness is sometimes thought of as doing the same thing over and over again and expecting a different result. I will not beat my head against a wall. If I am constantly misread and misunderstood somewhere, I will go elsewhere to see if I am understood there. I cannot come to see and understand myself if I am misunderstood and accused of being other than who I think and feel myself to be. I need to feel in synch enough to balance out one opinion with another, one perception with another. I will go crazy trying to get approval where it is constantly withheld. I need not overreact and run away in horror, but I definitely owe it to myself to get a second opinion. The truest home that I have is within me—where God and I dwell together.

Home is where the heart is.

Home is not where you live but where they understand you.

Christian Morgenstern

275

Love

If I were to choose one safe path to last me into forever, to lead me safely through this world, it would be the path of love. To love another, I first create that feeling within me (love doesn't come from nowhere). When I direct it outward, I generate it within me. I am at once the recipient and the sender, the giver and the receiver. Loving another allows me to love myself. It puts me in the space or path of love, it envelops me with the experience of love. Human love is the expression of soul on earth. It is the force that moves mountains, that turns plain and simple living into something noble and majestic. Love can make a pauper feel like a prince; lack of love can make a prince feel like a pauper. It is love that makes the difference between life feeling precious and valuable or worthless. I will get further in life by loving what I have than by looking forever elsewhere for meaning.

I will love what is near to me.

Love has power that dispels Death;
Charm that conquers the enemy.

Kahlil Gibran

▼

In the Heart of God

I will never be alone. No matter what happens in my life, no matter who comes and goes, I am not alone. I can reach into my inner depths and connect with the God that lives within and without me. I can move into the stillness of my own soul and be with all of creation, one with the infinite, one with God. I love this universe and it loves me. I am meant to be a part of the divine mystery. The heart of God is big enough to contain any and all of me—it accepts me as I am and I will do the same. My heart is big enough to join with the heart of God. I am carried always on the wings of spirit, I am safe in the loving hands of my Higher Power.

▼

I am not alone.

If you look for the truth outside yourself,
it gets farther and farther away.
Today walking alone, I meet (it) everywhere I step.
(It) is the same as me, yet I am not (it).
Only if you understand it in this way
will you merge with the way things are.

Tung-Shan

I Am Not My Roles

I have an identity behind the roles that I play in my life, a me that is constant, unchanging and connected to universal oneness or soul. Today I will allow myself to breathe deeply, detach from whatever role I am playing and rest in an eternal sense of self.

I am more than my roles.

The relative reality of these various identities (are) "real" only in relation to the situation which calls them forth. But if all of our identities are only relatively real, coming and going as circumstance warrants, is there any part of us that remains steady and stable behind all our roles? If we observe our own minds at work, we see that behind all these identities is a state of awareness that incorporates them all and yet is still able to rest behind them. As we loosen the hold of each identity so that we don't get completely lost in it, we are able to remain light and loose—able to play among these various aspects of being without identifying exclusively with any. We don't have to be anybody in particular. We don't have to be "this" or "that." We are free simply to be.

Ram Dass and Paul Gorman

▼

Care of the Soul

I will learn to see soul in everyday things. It is not life that needs to be different but my view of life. Little things, small soulful moments will catch my attention. I will see and notice soul's attempt to work its way into my day. I will allow the poet, the artist in me to come forth. After all, poetry and art begin in the mind. They are first and foremost a way of seeing, a method of synthesizing life. When I allow myself to be a poet or an artist, I combine the colors and impressions of my particular life in the manner that best suits me, that carries and communicates the most personal meaning.

▼

I will paint from my own palette.

Care of the soul is not solving the puzzle of life; quite the opposite, it is an appreciation of the paradoxical mysteries that blend light and darkness into the grandeur of what human life and culture can be. Let us imagine care of the soul, then, as an application of poetics to everyday life. What we want to do here is to re-imagine those things we already understand.

Thomas Moore

279

Soul as Nature

I will have proper reverence for all that is alive. When I lose my ability to respect and stand in awe of the mystery of life, I lose my soul along with it. I become a modern person in search of a soul, too often looking for it where it cannot be found. I become a feel-good person who constantly seeks that feeling of being "turned on" in order to feel connected to my own soul, my own aliveness. This is a setup for addiction—an invitation for every-*ism* to take over an empty place, then, eventually to take over me. Soul never left—I did. I will observe the process of soul, the process of life and living.

I see soul in all that lives.

Flower in the crannied wall,
I pluck you out of the crannies,
I hold you here, root and all, in my hand,
Little flower—but if I could understand
What you are, root and all, and all in all,
I should know what God and man is.

Alfred, Lord Tennyson

▼

Holistic Living

I am not merely an intellect—I am a body, mind and soul. When I divide myself into pieces, I do not function synergistically. If I am tired and stressed physically, I am not fully present. If my mind is tense and preoccupied, it takes my soul along with it. If my heart is heavy, the other parts of me follow suit. I cannot only think my way toward soul; I need to feel it, to sense and experience it with all of me. When I try to seek soul only through one sense or one function, I limit my potential.

▼

I function as a whole—all of me opens
to the soul experience.

In our souls everything
moves guided by a mysterious hand.
We know nothing of our own souls
that are ununderstandable and say nothing.

The deepest words
of the wise man teach us
the same as the whistle of the wind when it blows
or the sound of the water when it is flowing.

Antonio Machado

Home and Freedom

My home is a place of freedom and creativity. It is one place where I can be fully myself, where I can relax and let my hair down. My home holds within it a kind of comfort and safety that allows more of me to come forward. I can relax here, move about at my own pace, think my own thoughts, pursue my own quiet and pleasant routines. The world will not intrude upon this sacred space today—I will guard it with love, understanding its value to me. I have every right to protect my home from harm. This is my own cozy, little world and I will take care of it. I will not underestimate what it has to offer me.

I will live at home.

Of all modern notions, the worst is this: that domesticity is dull. Inside the home, they say, is dead, decorum and routine; outside is adventure and variety. But the truth is that the home is the only place of liberty, the only spot on earth where a man can alter arrangements suddenly, make an experiment or indulge in a whim. The home is not the only tame place in a world of adventure, it is the one wild place in a world of rules and set tasks.

C. K. Chesterton

Soul as Life

Soul is life, it is the energy that vivifies and animates. It is where all of me begins. When I take time in the quiet of my day to experience soul, I return to my own origins; I go within for nourishment and self-care. When I am stressed out or confused, it may just be that I am not structuring enough quiet time in my life, enough time to be refurbished through the silence of soul. Soul reveals itself to me in stillness. If I wish to know my own soul, I need to give myself daily quiet time, to contemplate, relax and just be. Without this quiet time, soul has no opportunity to emerge into my day. It is constantly kept beneath the surface, thwarted in its expression and expansion by business and preoccupation. Soul's expression comes when I sense its presence, when I am still enough to allow it to come forth. Soul is ever present in all things. Today I will remember to remember this truth.

Soul gives me movement and life.

For the soul is the beginning of all things. It is the soul that lends all things movement.

Plotinus

How Amazing Is This World

How fantastic it is to imagine a creator, a force behind this wondrous mystery of life. Could it really be possible? Could life and death still be life? Am I just another aspect of the cycle of life, of soul? Who is this power that creates such beauty? This mystery is beyond my powers of contemplation. It humbles me, it puts me into perspective, it makes everything else seem so much smaller. Life. Where do I begin to wonder about it? Is accepting the mystery enough or do I need to solve it in order to enjoy it? Perhaps I am only meant to accept and live with the mystery in order to participate, to stand in awe before that which I can probably never fully understand. Today, at least, that will have to do.

Today my jaw will drop.

What had that flower to do with being white,
The wayside blue and innocent heal-all?
What brought the kindred spider to that height,
Then steered the white moth thither in the night?
What but design of darkness to appall?—
If design govern in a thing so small

Robert Frost

Consistency

I will be consistent today. Soul cannot express itself and be explored through a chaotic, disorganized life. When I allow myself to be regular, to attend to the dailiness of a life's work, I create a work space within me for soul. Pursuing any one goal can get tedious and monotonous. Working through setbacks and frustrations can make me want to give up, to stop pushing, to abandon my mission. But it is by staying with it that I develop ego strength. It is in learning to tolerate small failures and frustrations that I build psychological and emotional muscle. This strength translates itself into an ability to handle the intensity of soul. Soul is a paradox, both exquisitely simple and maddeningly complex. It is necessary for me to develop strength of character in order to meet the inner challenges of a life aware of soul and spirit.

I will stay focused and committed
to a life's work.

Don't change horses in midstream.

Abraham Lincoln

285

The Dark Night of the Soul

Sharing my deepest shame helps me break out of my sense of isolation and disconnection from others. Secrets that I carry in the silence of my mind and heart divide me from myself and others. When I break my own silence, I crack the hard shell surrounding me and let in the light. I take a chance and trust other people with the banished contents of my mind, and being willing to trust another deepens my trust in myself. I learn that I can survive knowing and allowing others to know. Spirit cannot shine in darkness— it casts darkness away. A dark night of the soul can actually be part of letting in the light. Refused darkness is not light. Refused darkness actually blocks light from coming through. Honest pain and anguish are part of the process of soul growth, they are part of a willingness to grapple with and face the angst that blocks the spirit.

I will share with another what
I hold in silent shame.

Confession is good for the soul.

Scottish proverb

▼

Apology

I admire the person who can 'fess up to an error, take ownership of a personal shortcoming or apologize for a misstep. It lubricates my passage through life when I can own something and move on. If I have hurt someone or if my actions have caused a problem, it is up to me to come clean. Once I have done this, once I have attempted to make reparations, I have met someone halfway. At that time I need to give a person the time they need to do the same. I can only solve my end of a problem. When I try to reach into another's psyche and bear guilt and pain for that person as well as for me, I weaken us both and still come to no true resolution. I respect my own ability to make an apology and recognize that I have no control over another person. I will make my amends and leave your end of the problem for you to work through.

▼

I am capable of error and
capable of reparation.

None but a well-bred man knows how to confess a fault or acknowledge himself in an error.

Ben Franklin

Soul as Physician

Today I recognize that getting to know the soul within me is my best weapon against fatigue and depression. My circumstances may not change, but I experience my circumstances differently. I see life in a new way when soul is at the center of my being. All roads out of this center eventually refer back to soul, and are vivified by that energy. Living with soul as my center keeps my life in perspective. I see more clearly what is really important in life and what is of little consequence. Living with soul as my central point of reference keeps me connected to healing energy. It leads me to live with an attitude of health and aliveness in every cell. The cells of my body know what my attitude toward life is. Today I will teach them to live.

I connect from within.

A soul loss can be observed today as a psychological phenomenon in the everyday lives of the human beings around us. Loss of soul appears in the form of a sudden onset of apathy and listlessness; the joy has gone out of life, initiative is crippled, one feels empty, everything seems pointless.

Marie-Louise von Franz

Soul Refreshing

Soul is the life-spring within me from which I drink when I am thirsty. It is always willing to entertain another point of view, to take a fresh look, to forgive and try again. It is that bubbly, ebullient part of me that comes back for more, that recovers, that wakes into another morning with new energy. It is my soul that wishes to see meaning and beauty in my daily life. When I let myself feel and know that meaning, I am getting to know my own soul.

Soul is the spring from which I drink.

Soul sticks to the realm of experience and to reflections within experience. It moves indirectly in circular reasonings, where retreats are as important as advances, preferring labyrinths and corners, giving a metaphorical sense to life . . . Soul involves us in the pack and welter of phenomena and the flow of impressions. It is the "patient" part of us. Soul is vulnerable and suffers; it is passive and remembers. . . . The cooking vessel of the soul takes in everything, everything can become soul; and by taking into its imagination any and all events, psychic space grows.

James Hillman from *The Soul* by Phil Cousineau

Repositioning my Self

I will be willing to reposition myself today. When I lock myself into protective, defensive or aggressive poses, I am making any negotiating impossible. Being stubborn and clinging to my rigid position can be both dangerous and foolish. I can take another look.

I am willing to move and be moved.

Shortly after dark, the lookout on the wing of the bridge reported, "Light, bearing on the starboard bow."
"Is it steady or moving astern?" the captain called out.
Lookout replied, "Steady, captain," which meant we were on a dangerous collision course with that ship.
The captain then called to the signalman, "Signal that ship: We are on a collision course, advise you change course 20 degrees." Back came a signal, "Advisable for you to change course 20 degrees." The captain said, "Send, I'm a captain, change course 20 degrees." "I'm a seaman second class," came the reply. "You had better change course 20 degrees."
By that time, the captain was furious. He spat out, "Send, I'm a battleship. Change course 20 degrees."
Back came the flashing light, "I'm a lighthouse."
We changed course.

by Frank Koch from 7 *Habits of Highly Effective People*
by Steven J. Corey

Worship Without Words

I worship in silence, in the quiet sounds of nature. I am not guided by words and thoughts but by awe and wonder. I tune into the beauty that surrounds me. I see the true nature of soul and its many manifestations. Life beats a quiet drum beneath all that is apparent for me today. I listen, look, hear and see. I am part of the mystery.

I see soul in nature.

Like two cathedral towers these stately pines
Uplift their fretted summits tipped with cones;
The arch beneath them is not built with stones,
Not Art but Nature traced those lovely lines,
And carved this graceful arabesque of vines;
Listen! the choir is singing; all the birds,
In leafy galleries beneath the eaves,
Are singing! listen, ere the sound be fled,
And learn there may be worship without words.

Henry Wadsworth Longfellow

Center Stage

Though my movements may at times seem random and meaningless, I will trust that if I can tune into a force beyond me, my life will come to feel like a thousand meaningful coincidences with the deeper pulse of living. If I need scientific proof that all life is congruent and issues from one source, then that, too, is available. How much proof do I need to take the short step, the deep plunge into a life of soul awareness?

I look for and tune into a larger purpose.

Quantum physics brings us from the outskirts of reality to the center of the stage because we really do seem to play a fundamental role in the working of nature and this I find tremendously inspiring because it seems that my own individual life has more purpose; that the existence of mind and consciousness in the universe is in some sense meant to be. It's actually interwoven into the nature of reality in a very fundamental way. So in some sense we're not just a trivial add-on into the universe, not like extras that have stumbled onto the great cosmic set just by accident. We're truly written into the script, we're truly meant to be here.

Paul Davis

▼

A Better World

I have a vision of a better world. Today I will hold that vision in my heart and quietly move toward it. Anyone can say that the world is falling apart—why should I join them in that negative projection? It takes love and courage for me to see the world as basically good and to hold to that vision. When I see the world in a positive light, the world responds and my world becomes more positive. In this way I allow soul energy to manifest more fully and frequently in my life and in the world in which I live. I will believe in the world today with or without a good reason.

I will create a good world within me.

Let music for peace
Be the paradigm,
For peace means to change
At the right time. . . .
Making the flowing
Of time a growing,
Till what it could be
At last it is . . .

W. H. Auden
"Hymn to the United Nations"

Perpetual Morning

It is my fundamental nature to be always in a state of flux. My brain is elastic and ever young. I can and will tell myself a hundred times today that my brain has the ability to be ever flexible and open. Why should I atrophy, why should I decay psychologically? Life would be so much more pleasant if I felt young—not necessarily in years, but in spirit. I can be new each day. I can be new no matter how old I become. Today I will affirm my inner newness and openness over and over. Rather than slowly close, I will open; rather than decay, I will grow into new ways of living, new levels of experience.

To him whose elastic and vigorous thought
keeps pace with the sun, the day
is a perpetual morning.
Henry David Thoreau

The great art of life is knowing how to turn the surplus life of the soul into life for the body.

Henry David Thoreau

Personal Issues

I can come closer to my soul nature through rigorous psychological self-examination. Analyzing my drives and motivations or listening to the language of my dreams is a form of soul-searching. To ignore my personal self in my journey toward soul would be misguided; it would be a form of self-erasure. Grappling with my personal problems can be exasperating and frustrating, but it brings me closer to my inner being and allows me greater intimacy with soul.

I work with my personal issues.

Freud showed us how the soul could become aware of itself. To become acquainted with the lowest depth of soul—to explore whatever personal hell we may suffer from. . . . this demanding and potentially dangerous voyage of self-discovery will result in our becoming more fully human. Freud often spoke of the soul. . . . Unfortunately, nobody who reads him in English could guess this, because nearly all his many references to the soul, and to matters pertaining to the soul, have been excised in translation.

Bruno Bettleheim

Life Within

Just because I cannot see or sense the movement of spirit does not mean it isn't there. I will trust that it lies within all that I see, enlivening what seems motionless, giving beauty to what seems meaningless. Trust is built carefully over time. When I make the effort to notice spirit as it enters my day or tune in on it through quiet meditation, I am consciously building a trusting relationship with my own soul. I will not be fooled by appearances. The world around me is not hard, plastic and void of life—it is alive and filled with divine spirit.

There is life within what I see.

If we were not so single-minded
about keeping our lives moving,
and for once could do nothing,
perhaps a huge silence
might interrupt this sadness of never
understanding ourselves
and of threatening ourselves with death.

Perhaps the earth can teach us
as when everything seems to be dead in winter
and later proves to be alive.

Pablo Neruda

Creativity

I will follow my own creative path. When I am in touch with my own creativity, I am able to bring a creative eye to each and every day. Whether it be a dinner, a children's party or at work, creativity will breathe life and energy into the event. My creativity leads me to my spontaneity, which leads me to my ability to engage fully in the moment. Spontaneity has been defined by J.L. Moreno as an adequate response to a situation—adequate—no more or less than required, appropriate, natural and alive. Creativity and spontaneity connect my individual self with my higher self and the divine spirit energy.

I move with the flow of my own creativity.

Could Hamlet have been written by a committee, or the Mona Lisa painted by a club? Could the New Testament have been composed as a conference report? Creative ideas do not spring from groups. They spring from individuals. The divine spark leaps from the finger of God to the finger of Adam, whether it takes ultimate shape in a law of physics or a law of the land, a poem or a policy, a sonata or a mechanical computer.

A. Whitney Griswold

Hidden Beauty

What gives meaning to my life may lie beneath the surface. Today I will look not with my eyes but with my senses, to understand and experience what gives my life depth and importance. It is, at times, the promise of a hidden well that gives meaning to the surrounding atmosphere, the knowledge of a source of life that makes the day feel worthwhile and guides my mind closer to the mystery. Though I never hope to solve the mystery of life, sensing it will give my life a feeling of fullness. I am not here to explain but to experience life. Understanding comes more from direct experience than from collecting bits of knowledge.

I sense life's hidden meaning.

The desert is beautiful, the little prince added. And that was true. I have always loved the desert. One sits down on a desert sand dune, seeing nothing, hearing nothing. Yet through the silence something throbs, and gleams. . . . "What makes the desert beautiful," said the little prince, "is that somewhere it hides a well."

Antoine de St. Exupéry

October

The Golden God, the Self, the immortal Swan
   leaves the small nest of the body, goes
   where He wants.
He moves through the realm of dreams; makes
   numberless forms;
delights in sex; eats, drinks, laughs with His
   friends;
frightens Himself with scenes of heart-chilling
   terror.
But He is not attached to anything that He
   sees;
and after He has wandered in the realms of
   dream and awakeness,

has tasted pleasures and experienced good
   and evil,
He returns to the blissful state from which He
   began.
As a fish swims forward to one riverbank then
   the other,
Self alternates between awakeness and
   dreaming.
As an eagle, weary from long flight, folds its
   wings, gliding down to its nest,
Self hurries to the realm of dreamless sleep,
   free of desires, fear, pain,
As a man in sexual union with his beloved is
   unaware of anything outside or inside,
so a man in union with Self knows nothing,
   wants nothing,
has found his heart's fulfillment and is free of
   sorrow.
Father disappears, mother disappears, gods
   and scriptures disappear, thief disappears,
   murderer, rich man, beggar disappear,
   world disappears, good and evil disappear;
   he has passed beyond sorrow.

The Upanishads

▼

Sharing

I will share my joy with others. Simply living a happy life gives me much to pass around. Living well and happily is no small accomplishment. It means that I am doing something right, that I understand some basic truths about living and prospering in this world. Life is fundamentally simple, but recognizing this and actually simplifying my life requires a strong and mindful resolve, the strength of character to resist the complicated aspects of life that lead to self-destruction. What I have come to know through happy living are the profound lessons passed down through saints and sages. Appreciating joy in my life and sharing it with others enhances and increases its presence for me.

▼

I will share my joy.

Just as the wave cannot exist for itself, but is ever a part of the heaving surface of the ocean, so must I never live my life for itself, but always in the experience which is going on around me. It is uncomfortable doctrine which the true ethics whisper into my ear. You are happy, they say; therefore you are called upon to give much.

Albert Schweitzer

▼

Family Stories

My life is a journey, it is my story. Though it may not be recorded in history books, it has mythic proportions for me and for those close to me. Sharing personal stories enrich those who come after me. I am inspired and led by the stories of my elders. Family stories have special meaning because I feel the right to identify with them. They help me to know my own personal history, to write the book of *my* life. Each person in my family has traveled on his or her own journey, own vision quest. Hearing about how my relatives have sought meaning helps me have the courage to seek my own. The trail that they have blazed feels like mine to walk on and then to bequeath to my progeny.

I will listen to and share family stories.

In short, the soul-journey resembles very much the sort of adventure one encounters in folk lore and myth. According to archaic view, all men apparently had the chance to become a sort of Odysseus, whether they liked it or not.

Paul Zweig

Giving Back

Today, I will give back to the society in which I live. Looking for what I can do to make this a better world to live. It is soul in action. Spirit is not a stagnant thing, it is alive and moving. I cannot hold onto it or possess it. I need to flow with it, to co-create my day along with it through its spontaneous, moveable state. One of the easiest ways to have soul is to give it away. I cannot give anything that I am not also experiencing, and so in giving spirit and love away, I am also receiving it. Giving in this way gets the smaller me out of my own way so that I can experience the larger one, my transcendental self. The act of giving is an open path toward the soul experience. Paradoxically, giving may be the truest path toward receiving, the way that my humanness reaches toward spirit and clears the channels that carry soul's gifts.

I will look toward where I can be useful.

I sent my Soul through the Invisible,
Some letter of that After-life to spell,
And by and by my Soul returned to me,
And answered "I Myself am Heav'n and Hell."

Omar Khayyam

Recognizing Soul

I will not shrink from experiencing the ups and downs of my life. In the little disequilibrations of the day, soul energy is activated. Today I will pay attention. Rather than "get over it," I will "get into it." I will lengthen the moment of contact with my own individual soul. I get to know soul, cultivate and work with it in my own life by paying attention. My reactions, likes and dislikes map out my journey toward self. When I follow my own bliss, as it were, I am following me—I am moving in a direction of my own leaning, where more of me will be available to grow with and into; I am going with the flow of my own inner being and working with my intuitive self, the self that leads me toward soul.

I cultivate my own soul.

Every day, every more or less average human individual experiences the appearance of this energy in its most embryonic stage. Whenever there is pain or contradiction, this energy of the soul is released or "activated."

Jacob Needleman from *The Soul* by Phil Cousineau

Earthly Miracles

Every day the miracle of life renews itself. The earth restores itself. Life, in and of itself, is proof of the great, divine mystery, and the world in which I live is filled with wonder far beyond my comprehension. This day is living proof of the presence of soul.

I will contemplate the wonder.

If a dead man is raised to life, all men spring up in astonishment, yet every day one that had no being is born, and no man wonders, though it is plain to all, without doubt, that it is a greater thing for that to be created which was without being than for that which had being to be restored. . . . every day a tree is produced from the dry earth, and no man wonders. . . . Five thousand men were filled with five loaves . . . every day the grains of seed that are sown are multiplied in a fullness of ears, and no man wonders. . . . All wondered to see water once turned into wine. Every day the earth's moisture, being drawn into the root of the vine, is turned by the grape into wine, and no man wonders. Full of wonder then are all the things which men never think to wonder at, because . . . they are by habit become dull to the consideration of them.

Gregory the Great

▼

A Helpful Universe

Fearful as I can be of repeating painful history, it is important for me to understand that in a very fundamental way, it is impossible—the forces of nature are against it. In this alive world, billions of neurons are passing through each moment, altering the probabilities constantly. If I can release my self-defeating patterns, nature will do the rest. Dysfunctional patterns get passed on when I am in denial of my real self, when I can't look at and be with who I really am. If I was hurt by a certain behavior from someone as a child, I need to feel that hurt and own it as my own; otherwise, I will constantly see the world as *doing it to me*. I will project my pain and continually re-create the experience. There is no need for me to do this if I am willing to feel all my feelings surrounding a particular situation. This is my best weapon against repeating dysfunctional patterns. This teeming universe can come in and fill the vacuum created by my release and fill the space in me where an old wound used to be.

▼

The world will help me to heal.

You could not step twice in the same river.

Heraclitus

Easing Up

It is enough today to be alive, to wake up with a body full of energy, with senses that are in touch with the experience of living. I will eat my breakfast and enjoy it. I will walk, sit or listen to music. I will do whatever brings me pleasure and connects me with spirit. I choose not to pass hours of my day numb and dead inside, treating life as if it were worth nothing. Today I will be an appreciator of the ordinary. I will laugh at the apparent contradictions in events and the silliness of my own petty thoughts and actions. Today, wherever I am in my personal life is all right. I will not wish to be elsewhere. I will not hold myself and others to awful standards and postpone contented living pending my reaching some future goal. Today is all that I know I have. I will lighten up, loosen up and ease up.

I will relax and enjoy the ride.

Out-worn heart, in a time out-worn,
Come clear of the nets of wrong and right;
Laugh, heart, again in the gray twilight;
Sigh, heart, again in the dew of morn.

W. B. Yeats

Evolution of Spirit

I am part of a larger plan, the evolution of the human mind. If evolution is natural to the species of plants and animals, then I must be evolving as well. The true scholar seeks to build on what has been developed. He or she continues to test and prove, to grow theories and then to pass them on in good order to the next generation of researchers and learners. I will be a good scholar of life today, a competent researcher of the human soul. I will do my part to expand in the accumulated knowledge that I have access to, to experiment and add to a body of information and then to pass it lovingly on to the next generation.

I am part of the evolution of spirit.

"Cardinal Sebastian," he continued, "the Manuscript describes the progress of succeeding generations as an evolution of understanding, an evolution toward a higher spirituality and vibration. Each generation incorporates more energy and accumulates more truth and then passes that on to the people of the next generation who extend it further."

James Redfield, *The Celestine Prophecy*

▼

Inner Quiet

I create a pool of inner quiet through meditation and contemplation. I create a place of peace within me that I can call on throughout my day. I give myself time to sense the meaning of my life. Unless my mind slows down, I will not be still enough to *know through direct experience*. I will not have the inner peace to come in touch with deeper and deeper layers of self. If I accumulate and accomplish all that I set out to but lose my ability to enjoy, then I have bought into a fool's paradise. Then I will simply be surrounded by riches that I am unable to appreciate. I will take good care of myself today. I recognize that an important part of taking good care of myself is to give myself the quiet time I need and deserve in order to be happy.

▼

I give myself the quiet I need.

For what shall it profit a man, if he shall gain the whole world, and lose his own soul? Or what shall a man give in exchange for his soul?

Mark 8:36-37

▼

Shame

I will not hide my shame. All living persons, even animals, carry shame. It is a fundamental human feeling. When I carry shame in secret, it distorts my inner world. It makes me feel as if I have something bad inside of me that I need to keep hidden, something that, if it were known, would make people run away from or reject me. I build up resentment and fear; I even become paranoid imagining that people are saying and thinking things about me. Shame can make me lash out or act out; say and do things in an effort to get rid of the feeling. When I do this I only deepen my shame because only in owning and experiencing the feeling for what it is can I let it go.

▼

I feel and share shame.

We all carry shame, sharing it lightens the load and pulls it out of the secret undercurrents where it might get passed along in silence into the light of day where it can be seen for what it is. The more sinful and guilty a person tends to feel, the less chance there is that he will be a happy, healthy law abiding citizen. He will become a compulsive wrongdoer.

Dr. Albert Ellis

Plans

There is only one thing that I can expect from life with certainty, and that is change. When I realize this, the quality of my life is different. It acts as an intervention on my obsessive thinking. If I understand that I cannot count on my plans working out as I expect them to, perhaps I would be wise to plan differently. Having a plan is fine; it gives my day and life structure. However, when I think that a failed plan is a failed life, I get into trouble. Any good plan leaves room for chance, for the unexpected. It is when I want an event to match the image I have in my mind, or when I cannot leave room for chance, that I become controlling and upset. The world has too many variables for me to count on any one situation working out just as I expect it to; this type of expectation is a setup for disappointment. Today I will try something new, I will make a plan and then *let it happen.*

I expect the unexpected.

Nothing endures but change.

Heraclitus

311

Meaningful Actions

I will lose myself in a task today. Oftentimes I seek soul by sitting and ruminating in an effort to comprehend the mystery, but the self is too full of paradox to understand in any one way. Losing myself in meaningful activity is another way to journey toward soul. I thrive on a sense of accomplishment. I get a feeling of self-worth from applying my energies toward something worthwhile. Deepening and perfecting a skill lead me toward subtle levels of awareness and sharpen my powers of observation. Mixing and remixing my abilities, combining and recombining my approach to a task refine both my talent and level of awareness in any area of my inner or outer life. My life is made richer, fuller and more meaningful when I am able to devote my energies fully to worthwhile projects. Today I will see the value for me, in devoting myself to the task at hand.

I seek soul through devoted action.

In our world the road to holiness necessarily passes through the world of action.

Dag Hammarskjöld

Quiet Miracles

This world that I live in is filled with divine mystery. Each day I participate in quiet miracles that I don't even notice. I walk by the miracle of creation and the wonder of it remains unseen. Today, rather than live *mindlessly*, I will live *mindfully*. I will notice, I will see, I will touch and experience this wondrous world. I will quiet my mind and live in my body. I will be a part of the miracle.

I will take notice.

I like to walk alone on country paths, rice plants and wild grasses on both sides, putting each foot down on the earth in mindfulness, knowing that I walk on the wondrous earth. In such moments, existence is a miraculous and mysterious reality. People usually consider walking on water or in thin air a miracle. But I think the real miracle is not to walk either on water or in thin air, but to walk on earth. Every day we are engaged in a miracle which we don't even recognize.

Thich Nhat Hanh

Inner Conflict

Soul is not some disembodied entity—it is part of me, part of my struggle. When I bring deep conflicts housed in my unconscious to a conscious level, I am making more of soul conscious as well. Every aspect of life or thought has soul present within it. Conflict that is locked in a frozen state in my deeper mind locks soul along with it. To free my mind also frees soul and life energy. Soul is a mighty phenomenon, as big as all creation. I need to expand my mind to be able to contain it or be with it.

I study inner conflicts to expand my soul.

To experience conflicts knowingly, though it may be distressing, can be an invaluable asset. The more we face our own conflicts and seek out our own solutions, the more inner freedom and strength we will gain. Only when we are willing to bear the brunt can we approximate the ideal of being the captain of our ship. Spurious tranquillity rooted in inner dullness is anything but enviable. It is bound to make us weak and an easy prey to any kind of influence.

Karen Horney, M.D.

The Study of Nature

Each and every person is an artist or a scientist in their own way. I create myself through observation of life and self, then I individualize and apply what I learn. In this way I create myself and my life. I will keep this in mind today. I will ask myself how I can perceive and interact with my day to deepen my understanding of myself and my world. In addition, I will see what creative solutions I can come up with to solve little tasks throughout my day. I may try something as small as driving a different way to work or planning a different outing than usual, or as large as envisioning a new life endeavor. I will use my intuition to inform my process of decisionmaking and give it my own creative spin. I am the artist and my life is my canvas.

I am an artist and a scientist.

The whole secret in the study of nature lies in learning how to use one's eyes.

George Sand

Masculine and Feminine

I have two aspects: the masculine and the feminine, the animus and anima. Both male and female unite within me. I will bring both these parts of myself into balance because it is important to my mental health. I can be intuitive and nurturing simultaneously with allowing for healthy aggression and competence. I am biologically equipped for all of these characteristics to varying degrees. Today's world requires that I be actively in touch with all these qualities—every one of them is important if I wish to be the kind of person that modern lifestyles require. When I feel myself getting out of balance, I will set about restoring the qualities within me and within my day that I am missing.

I am the masculine and the feminine.

This marriage of the masculine with the feminine has to take place in all of our hearts and minds, whether we are male or female. The mystical and practical health it brings is the goal of being human, the basis and energy of all true transformation.

Andrew Harvey

▼

Death

I daily entertain my own death. My days here are limited. I do not have time to waste in hating and resenting life. I will never again be in this particular circumstance as this particular person. If I waste it, it is gone. All the lessons that I need to know in order to grow spiritually are written into this present moment. The people and situations that are in my life are here for me to learn from. They are meant for me. My deepest learnings are at the tips of my fingers. I will be a scholar of life, a student of my day. My own death waits for me at a time unknown. I will live today as if it were my last—every day potentially is.

▼

I am aware.

Only those are fit to live who do not fear to die; and none are fit to die who have shrunk from the joy of life and the duty of life. Both life and death are parts of the same great adventure.

Theodore Roosevelt

My Animal Nature

I will not resist my animal nature today. If I am truly a part of a divine plan, then all of me is meant to be here, both my animal and spirit sides have soul potential encoded into them. I will not sever myself from my own humanity in order to become something beyond myself—my *becoming* is in my *being*, my soul and my person are of the same stuff.

I balance my physical and soul nature.

I don't think I can learn from a wild animal how to live in particular—shall I suck warm blood, hold my tail high, walk with my footprints precisely over the prints of my hands?—but I might learn something of mindlessness, something of the purity of living in the physical senses and the dignity of living without bias or motive. The weasel lives in necessity and we live in choice, hating necessity and dying at the last ignobly in its talons. I would like to live as I should, as the weasel lives as he should. And I suspect that for me the way is like the weasel's: open to time and death painlessly, noticing everything, remembering nothing, choosing the given with a fierce and pointed will.

Annie Dillard

▼

Opening to Soul

I will open my self to the soul experience today. Both on an individual and a universal level, soul is there waiting for me to let it in. This is my birthright, just as the air and the sun are as much mine as anyone's—soul is here for me. There is no price tag on soul, no being good enough in the eyes of the world to finally deserve it. All that is required is a recognition and a willingness to allow soul energy into my life and heart, into my being.

For me to understand that soul is available to me at all times requires a paradigm shift. It asks me to *see* differently—to look for and identify the mystery of soul in the world as it is, to see unity in diversity and perfection in what is apparently imperfect. Understanding soul asks me to look behind the thin veil of reality and glimpse the infinite.

▼

I will experience soul.

That which oppresses me, is it my soul trying to come out in the open, or the soul of the world knocking at my heart for its entrance?

Rabindranath Tagore

▼

Time and Space

I will look beyond time and space into the infinite nature of the universe, into soul. What I see around me is not all there is to this world. Call me crazy, but I see more. I trust my eyes and I trust my heart. What I see with my mind and my heart are just as real for me as what I see with my eyes. Reality is multi-layered. When I am still and quiet it unfolds itself to me. Its wisdom and meaning seep effortlessly into my pores. I come to understand truth and soul because I sense its presence within me. I am a part of this divine mystery of life. I am indivisible with the whole, a cog in an ever-turning wheel of time, beyond which lies eternity, more life, more me, more it.

▼

I see beyond time and space.

The influence of the senses has in most men overpowered the mind to that degree that the walls of time and space have come to look real and insurmountable; and to speak with levity of these limits is, in this world, the sign of insanity. Yet time and space are but inverse measures of the force of the soul.

Ralph Waldo Emerson

Prayer

Today I pray with the full, unseparated power of God within me. I am one with spirit. When I align myself with the God-force that is present and alive in all things, my prayer has meaning and strength. When I pray to the God-center of my being, I bring a troubled spirit in touch with the light of God. When I pray with full faith that this universe is meant for me and those in it, with a genuine awareness that God and I are one, that there is no separation, then I place my hand on the switch that has power and light behind it. Prayer is dynamic. It speaks to the benevolent force of love and creativity that brings life to this world. I will pray each day, knowing that my prayers are meant to be fulfilled.

I acknowledge the power of sincere prayer.

Ask, and it shall be given you; seek, and ye shall find; knock, and it shall be opened unto you.

Matthew 7:7

Giving

I will open my life to the act of giving today. Giving and receiving are the same channel. When I am able to truly give, I have tuned into the channel, opened the pipeline, through which I receive. When I love another, I am loving the self—giving and receiving love. The act of giving is the key. In giving I receive, in loving I open to experience love—the world is impartial. If I open the vessel of me, it will be filled.

I give and I love.

The essential truth about the existence of man is in the Gospels. What we are, what we hope, what we need, is contained in the Gospels. But they can be difficult. An easier bridge to their meaning is St. Francis of Assisi. Simply, Saint Francis says the key to the purpose of life is giving. In giving, you find happiness. You find peace. If you give, you find you are serving your purpose in life. In loving, you find love.

Franco Zeffirelli from *The Meaning of Life*

Maturity

I can keep myself in perspective. I have been around the block with myself many times. I know where I get snagged up, I know where certain relationships or circumstances will lead me. I am familiar with how I react to various circumstances. Just for today, I will avoid going down a street that I know is filled with potholes and will take a street that runs some other way. Why should I deliberately set myself up for disappointment when I can just as easily avoid it? Why should I do what I know will not yield high returns? If I know and understand myself, then it is my responsibility to put that knowledge to good use, to allow it to steer me through my life in positive and pleasant ways. My life works better when I am able to witness myself in action, knowing that I can enter in by choice rather than compulsion, feeling free to act as I choose, to tailor my life to suit me.

I act with maturity.

Maturity consists in no longer being taken in by oneself.

Kajetan von Schlaggenberg

▼

Crazy Wisdom

I will relax and let it happen. I will be open to new forms of thinking, being and learning. This world is changing rapidly, and part of my keeping up with the times will simply lie in my ability to float with and toward new states of awareness. I will open my mind to something new today.

▼

I am alive at an exciting time.

If you find it hard to keep up with all the new scientific breakthroughs, you might find solace in the "hundredth monkey" theory. Although widely disputed, it claims that if enough members of a species learn something new, a point of saturation is reached whereupon the entire species will begin to understand it spontaneously. Biologist Rupert Sheldrake formulated a hypothesis . . . that new behaviors or concepts can spread through a species spontaneously, due to a vibratory process called "morphic resonance." Practically speaking, this means that if we just relax and wait awhile, enough people will read up on the idea of morphic resonance, and we won't have to. Sometimes it is okay to let ourselves be monkey number one hundred one. Crazy wisdom says, "Let's take turns."

Wes Nisker

Re-Experiencing Trauma

If I have been deeply upset or traumatized by something, I may be hiding an unhealed wound in my unconscious. While I was originally experiencing the trauma, my reaction may have been *fight, flight or freeze*. All these were natural reactions, part of being a human animal; none allowed me to be *in* the situation and process it cognitively or emotionally.

Unprocessed experience gets stored in a sort of flash-frozen state. When it gets triggered by a current life event, it begins to thaw out and to hurt; it may cause me to over-react either inside myself or through my actions. Today when this happens I will ask myself if my deep emotional reaction to a situation is appropriate or if an old wound is getting pressed. If it is an old wound, I will let myself feel it and become aware of how that old pain is affecting me in my life today.

I find freedom through healing trauma.

Truly one learns only by sorrow; it is a terrible education that the soul gets and it requires a terrible grief that shakes the very foundation of one's being to bring the soul into its own.

British Major Lanoe Hawker, V.C.

Self-Study

I can deepen in my knowledge of God—in fact, I am meant to do just that. The sphere of God consciousness is part of the mystery of life, the mystery of me. One of the vehicles I have been given through which to learn is my mind and the way that my mind interprets my personal experience. My life is my *experience* of my life, my interpretation. My life has meaning and beauty to the extent that I possess those qualities. I see from within. I am an heuristic study of soul. By studying myself, I study the mysteries of the All-Soul. Through rigorous self-honesty and an open attitude toward what is really going on inside me, I can study humankind. I am a piece of the mystery—in learning about me, I learn about the deeper layers of the universe.

I will study myself.

God is an intelligible sphere known to the mind—each of us is a part of that mystery.

Joseph Campbell

Soul and Selfishness

Soul is non-material. It is not a thing to be won or bought or sold. It is not something that I can wrap my intellect around and finally grasp by breaking it down into small parts. Soul isn't a reward that someone will give me if I am good enough, an accolade I can earn by being smart enough, or an object I can collect when I am rich enough. Soul is an experience that requires that I am willing and able to drop into *me,* to touch the divine spark within, to nurture my own spirit. Soul is that place where all the waters meet, where giving and receiving are one, where deep letting go and release happen and where ego and vanity disappear. Where soul goes, selfishness does not, and where selfishness goes, soul does not.

I open my heart to soul.

The word soul with us seems to be synonymous with stomach. We plead and speak not as from the soul but from the stomach. *We plead not for God's justice, (but) for our own interests, our rents and profits.*

Thomas Carlyle

Living Once

This will be my only lifetime as the person I am today. I will only pass through this day once. What I do with this day I will only be able to do once. If I waste the entire day, it will be a day wasted; if I walk blindly through it, it will be a day unseen; if I hate it, dread it or wish it away, it will be recorded in my brain as a terrible day. In any case, I will never have this day back to do over again. How I conduct myself in it will be all that I have to carry away with me; how the way that the moment transpires will be what is written into the diary of my personal experience, the diary contained within my mind.

This is my only opportunity to live this day.

Through this toilsome world, alas!
Once and only once I pass;
If a kindness I may show,
If a good deed I may do
To a suffering fellow man,
Let me do it while I can.
No delay, for it is plain
I shall not pass this way again.

Author unknown

▼

Mind-Body Connection

My state of mind affects my body. Wherever thought travels, a chemical travels with it. The chemicals in my body are then affected by my thoughts. This means that who I am on the inside affects who I am on the outside. I am not just guessing at this, it is not some New Age notion that neurochemical and physical makeup are interconnected. My state of mind and my level of inner spirit have the power to impact and improve me physically. Today I will affirm within me that I have a beautiful and healthy body and mind. I will thank a Higher Power for giving me a healthy, strong and beautiful body. I will do this as often as I can remember to do it throughout my day.

▼

My body is beautiful, strong and healthy.

The same is true of the face, which is shaped and formed according to the content of the mind and soul, and the same is again true of the proportions of the human body. Thus can this member of astronomy describe each kind of soul. For the sculptor of Nature is so artful that he does not fashion the soul to fit the form, but the form to fit the soul.

Paracelsus, 16th century physician, alchemist

Silent Communication

I am not an island onto myself. Isolating myself from those I am intimate with is impossible. All I accomplish through this self-imposed separation is the illusion of isolation. I share space with those who are close to me. Each of us knows what is going on, each of us feels the atmosphere of the other. I will be willing to know how I affect people today on both a verbal and, even more important, on a nonverbal level. I will take responsibility not only for what I say, but for who I am in the alive and vibrating feeling atmosphere around me. The atmosphere around me is alive and carries my silent message to all whom I encounter; it is what others I am in relationship with know and live with.

I own what I think and feel.

Now if you apply the wave-particle metaphor to human relationship and think that we are both particle, individuals in our own space and time and waves, things that can overlap and combine with others, then you have a basis for seeing how we could get "into" relationships with other people.

Dianne Zohar

Primitive Soul

I am more than my mind and body. They will some day die, pass into another form—but the soul within me was, is and always will be part of eternity. My deep unconscious self has more power to shape me than I realize. I depend on it for my day-to-day functioning. My unconscious contains all my accumulated experience and connects me to the deeper aspects of the world and universe in which I live.

I am connected with forever.

Actually, however, we are dependent to a startling degree upon the proper functioning of the unconscious psyche and must trust that it does not fail us. . . .
Experience shows us that the sense of the "I"—the ego-consciousness—grows out of unconscious life. The small child has psychic life without any demonstrable ego-consciousness, for which the earliest years leave hardly any traces in memory. Where do all our good and help-ful flashes of intelligence come from? What is the source of our enthusiasms, inspirations, and of our heightened feeling for life? The primitive senses in the depths of his soul the springs of life.

Carl Jung

November

The President in Washington sends word that he wishes to buy our land but how can you buy or sell the sky, the land, the idea is strange to us. Every part of this earth is sacred to my people. Every shining pine needle, every sandy shore. Every mist in the dark woods, every meadow. All are holy in the memory and experience of my people. We're part of the earth and it is part of us. The perfumed flowers are our sisters. The bear, the deer, the great eagle, these are our brothers. Each ghostly reflection in the clear water tells of events and memories in the life of my people. The water's murmur is the voice of my father's father. The rivers are our brothers, they carry our canoes and feed our children. If we sell you our land remember that the air is precious to us, that the air shares its spirit with the life that supports us. The wind that gave our grandfather his first breath also receives his last sigh.

This we know, the earth does not belong to man. Man belongs to the earth, all things are connected like the blood that unites us all, man did not weave the web of life he is only a strand in it, whatever he does to the web, he does to himself. Your destiny is a mystery to us, what will happen when the buffalo are all slaughtered, what will happen when the secret corners of the forest are heavy with the scent of many men, when the views of the ripe hills are blotted with talking wires? The end of living and the beginning of survival, when the last red man has vanished with his wilderness and his memory is only a cloud moving across the prairie, will these shores and forests still be here? Will there be any spirit of my people left?

We love this earth as a newborn loves his mother's heartbeat. So if we sell you our land, love it as we've loved it, care for it as we've cared for it, hold in your mind the memory of the land as it is when you receive it. Preserve the land for all children and love it as God loves us all. One thing we know, there's only one God, no man be he red man or white man can be apart. We are brothers after all.

Chief Seattle, 1852

My Own Point of View

In my quiet moments I allow myself to fully entertain my own thoughts. I learn and grow in layers. When I have come finally to decode what feels like garbled data and to understand more clearly what I am seeing, feeling and hearing, then I am ready to move through another layer. Some days, learning how to live feels like too hard a struggle, but then I consider the alternatives—living a hollow and meaningless life, wasting or even resenting life, living stupidly and blundering mindlessly along, living only on the surface, never letting anything or anyone really touch or move me is certainly no easier. When I consider the alternatives, it puts the struggle in perspective; I understand why I carry on.

The struggle is worthwhile.

We do not receive wisdom, we must discover it for ourselves, after a journey through the wilderness which no one else can make for us, which no one can spare us, for our wisdom is the point of view from which we come at last to regard the world.

Marcel Proust

Living with Death

Death is the other side of life—it is with me all the time. I could die at any moment. It is the one thing in my life that I have no control over. It waits for me at a distance unknown. It is inevitable. Knowing death waits for me makes life all the more real and three-dimensional. There is great comfort just in being alive.

I am alive today.

"You must agree, Don Juan, not thinking about death certainly protects us from worrying about it."

"Yes, it serves that purpose," he conceded. "But that purpose is an unworthy one for average men and a travesty for sorcerers. Without a clear view of death, there is no order, no sobriety, no beauty. Sorcerers struggle to gain this crucial insight in order to help them realize at the deepest possible level that they have no assurance whatsoever their lives will continue beyond the moment. That realization gives sorcerers the courage to be patient and yet take action, courage to be acquiescent without being stupid."

Carlos Castaneda

Denial of Fear

If I hurt, today I can own it and if I am afraid, I can admit rather than hide it. Experiencing my own fear can make me so anxious that I try to pretend it isn't there. This is when I look for crutches to hold me up. Owning my own fear actually gives me strength. It allows me not to be caught off guard or get overly triggered by whatever frightens me. When I know I am afraid, I have a stronger psychological position than when I deny that part of myself.

It's okay for me to be afraid.

[We] *frame the situation in such a way that we can once again open ourselves to new possibilities of response to suffering. They can turn our attention to an examination of the reactions that suffering triggers off in us. Up to now these reactions have been rooted not only in fear but in the denial of fear. Merely to be mindful of this pattern is to be one step closer to our own truth and, in turn, to the truth of someone else's suffering. Truth is where we will meet. Simply acknowledging our reactiveness to pain, therefore, is itself an initial act of service.*

Ram Dass and Paul Gorman from *How Can I Help?*

Seeing Soul in the Simple

I will look forward to the beauty and meaning that is present within simple, everyday life situations. This world is extraordinary, but I have to come to take it for granted. The miracle of life, of the sea, the skies, the beauty of a sunset of flowers and trees—the majesty of birth, love and creativity. All of these surround me on a daily basis, yet I walk right by them as if they contained no mystery, no magic, no soul. If I want to see soul, I will start where I am. From this moment on, I will learn to see rather than search. It is all right here, it always was—I just need to recognize it.

I see soul in the ordinary.

When you see ordinary situations with extraordinary insight, it is like discovering a jewel in rubbish.

Chögyan Trungpa

Expectations

When I postpone living until I am perfect, all I accomplish is that I don't really live. I miss the moment, I lose the day. They say that expectations can be premeditated resentments. Perfection is an illusion, enlightenment will not mean a perfect, pain-free life, even to want that is a sort of flight from what is real and alive. Life holds no promises for me or anyone else. I will do my part and appreciate the life that I have been given. So much of enlightenment is in my ability to see and perceive. In order to see clearly, I need to clean my inner lens, to sort out distortions and to work through personal baggage. What I believe to be true about anyone or anything is possible also about me. If happiness exists for someone else, it can exist for me, and vice versa.

Life is enough.

Before enlightenment, carry the water, till the soil.
After enlightenment, carry the water, till the soil.

Zen proverb

▼

My Own Path

I am on my own, individualized path through life, I am unique. I am not in a position to judge another person nor should I take others' judgments of me too much to heart. There have been so many tiny variables that have gone into shaping who I am—my path has been my own and all those around me have a path that is their own. I cannot really judge another person because I could not possibly have enough information to truly see the whole story, to understand in full and fair measure just what has gone into making another person tick. It is difficult enough to understand myself. Why do I feel I am so capable of judging another fairly?

▼

I honor my own unique experience.

The six tips of a single snowflake . . . feel the same temperatures, and because the laws of growth are purely deterministic, they maintain a near-perfect symmetry. But the nature of turbulent air is such that any pair of snowflakes will experience very different paths. The final flake records the history of all the changing weather conditions it has experienced, and the combinations may as well be infinite.

James Gleick

Over Identification

I will be cognizant of the birth experience constantly taking place in my mind. My internal reaction to the thoughts that arise in my mind is what defines my inner experience, which, in turn, becomes my will toward living.

I will be conscious of my mental reactions.

A "birth" experience occurs when consciousness contacts an object. In Vipassana terms, "birth" means that a new situation is emerging in the mind. It is similar to match and flint coming together. Fire arises when contact occurs between them (touching and striking action). Inattention to contact gives Ignorance (not-knowing) a chance to surface. As soon as sense contact with an object arises, sensation (pleasant, unpleasant, or neutral) appears at once. Contact immediately causes a reaching out, a grasping and clinging to the object. When we are unmindful and delusion arises. Ignorance conditions mental formations which, in turn, conditions volition. When grasping and clinging are halted, there is no longer a condition for the arising of imbalance manifesting as desire or aversion.

Sri Aurobindo

Soul in the Natural World

Today I entertain the possibility that each and every living thing carries and is made up of the soul force. Soul is genderless and shapeless, a part of the air, a bird or an animal, it runs through forested ground. Soul is life. My individual soul is an expression of the All-Soul but why not the fallen log and the leaves that rustle in the breeze? Why shouldn't all that is living contain soul and in some form express it. When I perceive the world as being manifestations of soul, I begin to see it differently, to value it anew. The world becomes as Martin Buber would say, a thou rather than an it, alive rather than dead. When the world is a thou I connect with it and engage with it rather than manage and move it mindlessly around. I see the world as a thou today, alive and awake.

▼

The world is alive.

In addition to souls which run and shriek and devour, might there not be souls which bloom in stillness, exhale fragrance and satisfy their thirst with dew and their impulses by their burgeoning?

Peter Tompkins and Christopher Bird

Human Love

Human love is alive with the force of soul. In and through this love I connect with my higher self, with transcendent experience: the temporal becomes divine. Human love is a spiritual gift, frightening in its power, devastating when lost. It is the bridge over which spirit moves toward flesh, a container of divine energy, a force that has the power to fight darkness with warmth and light. Human love and relationship are what make the world go round. I will not lose faith in people. Today I will open myself to giving and receiving love. I will make pleasant and meaningful contact with others. I will not hold back.

I believe in the power of love.

The pleasure of life is in loving,
and we are made happier by the passion that
we experience
than by that which we inspire.

La Rochefoucauld

Letting Go

For centuries, jungle dwellers have captured monkeys in this way: they make clay pots with long thin necks and a round base large enough to hold a banana on its side. Monkeys in search of food reach down and grab hold of the banana. Once they have their banana, they have two choices: they can keep hold of it, trying over and over to pull it out of an impassable spout, or they can let the banana go.

How often do I trap myself in this same way? By refusing to let go of the promise of something that I can touch but not have, I become caught in the action of pulling on life to give me an experience that may never be mine. Because I cannot let go of the wish for something, I am captured, I am at the mercy of another whether it be a person, society, or the media; my boat is steered along someone else's course. Letting go of that which has me in its grip releases my soul from the captivity of the preoccupations of my mind. Sometimes what I feel I have hold of actually has hold of me.

I will let go.

None but a fool worries about what he cannot influence.

Samuel Johnson

Soul's Subtle Presence

This world seems to be composed of countless separate objects, but if I look I will learn to see soul within them. What gives this world life is the one energy of soul alive in all that I see. There is a creative intelligence dispersed with all that is alive. So refined is this divine intelligence that it is subtle enough to be present and alive in each particle, in each living thing. Today when I look at a tree or a flower or the face of a person, I will see an expression of soul.

I see soul's presence in all that is living.

We live in succession, in division, in parts, in particles. Meantime within man is the soul of the whole; the wise silence; the universal beauty, to which every part and particle is equally related; the eternal ONE. And this deep power in which we exist and whose beatitude is all accessible to us is not only self-sufficing and perfect in every hour, but the act of seeing and the thing seen, the seer and the spectacle, the subject and the object, are one. We see the world piece by piece, as the sun, the moon, the animal, the tree; but the whole, of which these are the shining parts, is the soul.

Ralph Waldo Emerson

Beyond Darkness

The energy of soul is present in all that exists. For centuries people have recognized this basic life truth. It is not soul or eternal self that gets lost, it is me. I will make it a point today to see soul where it is present in my day. I will consciously look for it and attempt to feel it and notice its expression. Soul energy is synonymous with life energy. It breathes life into this world. It both leads and guides, quietly abiding in all that is. I will suspend my disbelief. Today I will take a leap of faith and reach across the great darkness within me to unite with and recognize the face of soul.

I cross the farther shore beyond darkness.

Where the channels are brought together
Like the spokes in the hub of a wheel—
Therein he moves about,
Becoming manifold.
Om!—Thus meditate upon the Soul (Atman).
Success to you in crossing to the farther
shore beyond darkness!

The Second Khanda Upanishad

Having a Dream

I will imagine a dream fulfilled right now, this moment. I will see the table prepared before me. Life means to support me in the realization of my desires. It will move in and help if I can truly allow myself to see and feel that what I wish for as possible and indeed ready to be. Over and over again, I will visualize the circumstance that I wish to have in my life. I will mentally interact with it as if it were real. I will accept it as possible for me as if it were actually happening right now. Then I will let it go. I will see in my mind what I wish to see manifest in my life.

I will dream today.

The essential process behind positive thinking is first to set yourself goals and then to imagine them having been achieved. It is not just a question of setting goals, but of seeing in your mind's eye, the goals being fulfilled. The importance of this can be understood in terms of mental set. . . . Imagining as strongly as possible, the fulfillment of your dreams as already having occurred, sets you positively for events and opportunities that will support your goals.

Peter Russell, *The Brain Book*

Celebrating a Ritual

Ritual offers a vehicle through which to connect with my self, my community and my ancestral inheritance. It creates a container through which communal spirit can come forward and be experienced. Ritual provides a passageway for the collective consciousness to express itself and be felt. It operates on a variety of levels and offers a secure, concrete structure that invites the self and the soul to come forward into the day. What often might go unseen or unfelt has a place to be. It has a moment carved out in space and time where it can inspire both individuals and the group, and where it can act as a reminder that life is more than we see.

I want ritual in my life because it steadies me. It connects me with a community and helps that community to connect with its own roots, traditions and collective meaning. Rituals help me to experience continuity in my life.

I respect and maintain rituals.

It is superstition to put one's hope in formalities; but it is pride to be unwilling to submit to them.

Pascal

Constructive Activity

I will do something constructive with my day. Sitting back and watching my day disappear will not give me a good feeling about myself when I lay my head down on my pillow tonight. There is always something constructive to do in any given day. Today I will do it, not procrastinate—I will do it. I may clean out a closet, write correspondence, exercise or take on a new project—whatever it is, I will start now. Constructive activity creates a pathway for the soul, it builds on strength and positivity. Self-esteem comes from feeling myself to be a useful and valuable person. When I am not constructive in my day, I rob myself of that important source of self-confidence and self-competence; then I am prey to negative influences. If I wish to feel like a useful, vital person, I will need to act like one.

I begin a constructive activity now.

Three are three gates to . . . death of the soul:
The gate of lust.
The gate of wrath.
The gate of greed.

Bhagavad-Gita

Engagement

I will engage in the process of living today. Thinking about life is not living it. Jane Austin referred in her writing to "the healing waters of action." Participation in living is the key to feeling a part of the world, valuable, seen, heard and known. When I withdraw from the world, I withdraw from soul because the world is of the spirit. Being a part of the process of living is being and growing with spirit. Times of quiet and meditation are not dropping out of life—rather, they are dropping into it, contacting it at a deeper level. Withdrawing or hiding are altogether different and tend to be fear-based actions. Participation is forward-moving and interactive. It gives life a feeling of buoyancy and purpose. I will engage fully in my day today in whatever it is that I do.

I am a participator.

The end of man is to let the spirit in him permeate his whole being, his soul, flesh, and affections. He attains his deepest self by losing his selfish ego.

Robert Musil

Soul Aborted

This energy of soul is alive and available, but I cut it off in a thousand little ways. Today instead of blocking the entering of soul energy into my life, I will invite it. I will not retreat from soul's intent to evidence itself in my day. I will instead learn to read the circumstances and coincidences of my day as a student researching the many varied ways that the spark of spirit enters my life. I will study the manifestation of soul through daily events.

I open the door for soul energy.

Whenever there is pain or contradiction, this energy of the soul is released or "activated." But almost always, almost without any exceptions whatsoever, this new energy is immediately dispersed and comes to nothing. A hundred, a thousand times a day, perhaps, "the soul is aborted." An individual is completely unaware of this loss and remains so throughout his whole life. . . . "Lost Christianity" is the lost or forgotten power of man to extract the pure energy of the soul from the experiences that make up his life.

Jacob Needleman

351

Solving Today

I only need to solve today. How much of my precious time and energy do I use up on trying to solve my life months and years from now? While it is important that I live prudently and intelligently so as to plan responsibly for my future, it is equally important that I recognize that today well-lived is the foundation upon which I build my tomorrow.

The life I am so busy planning and worrying about will likely not be as I imagine it. I will have forgotten something or an unforeseen circumstance will alter my plan. Did I know ten years ago that this is what I would be doing now? If only I could let go of the constant low level of anxiety about my unknown future, I am sure today would feel longer, deeper and less complicated. I can only solve today—it is the only time that is actually within my reach.

I will live in the present moment.

What they undertook to do
They brought to pass;
All things hang like a drop of dew
Upon a blade of grass

W. B. Yeats

▼

Forgiveness

Forgiveness is what enables a person to become whole again rather than to live broken. It is perhaps a moment when we choose or, by seeming coincidence meet choice along life's path between neurosis and spiritual growth; a moment when the spirit guides the flesh.

▼

I forgive someone who has hurt me.

A middle-aged man came to place his child in one of my classes, but I realized I had no room at all. I looked at this man and immediately knew. This was the guard who had beaten me nine years before.

A spirit caught me. I understood that I had to find space for his boy. I could not repeat the harm that had been done to me. I asked him, "Do you know me?" He said, "No." I asked him if he remembered a night in July of 1956. Just then, the man looked at my face and started crying. He began to walk away, but I stopped him, saying, "Wait, I'll take the child. I have carried scars for years, but I have forgiven you all those things." That man might have left me permanently disabled, but in allowing me to help his boy, he made me feel fulfilled in what I wanted to do for young people.

Joel Kinagwi, *The Meaning of Life*

Being True to my Values

Today I will remember that if I wish to feel congruent and whole on the inside, I need to lead a life that reflects my values and is true to who I am. When I think and feel in one way but structure my life in another, I feel out of sync. Honesty is not only expressed in words, but is also present in how I live. The most important and powerful aspects of honesty will evidence themselves not in what I say but in what I do. It is my behavior and the way in which I live that is the outward expression of my inner values. My personal integrity is simply living in a way that honors who I feel I am on the inside, that goes with rather than against my values, my dreams and talents.

I will live close to who I am.

Self-respect at the highest levels comes from honoring your soul. This means speaking and acting from a level of integrity and honesty that reflects your higher self. It means standing by what you believe in (you don't, however, have to convince others to believe in it), and acting in a way that reflects your values.

Sanaya Roman

▼

My Own Light

There is a light within me that waits quietly to be discovered. The more I can accept and spend time with that inner well of light, the more it will shine through me into this world. I am a channel for, and a carrier of, soul's light. This light is universal, it belongs to no one and can be accessed by anyone. When I spend time in the space of my own inner light, I nourish the very cells of my body, I revive and refresh all of me. This is how I set myself up to enjoy life. It puts me in a position to enjoy the things and experiences of the world without looking to them to heal me or bring love into my life. Love and light can pass through me, through that core of me that connects to all that is, was and ever will be.

▼

I have light within me.

The discovery of your own reality, your own light, will not fit into anything. But, it will affect everything. Something happens upon the planet when one man comes to that state. He has nothing to preach for he is a light unto himself. So can you be.

Tara Singh

Personal Responsibility

Today I will take responsibility for the condition of my life. The thought of doing this is both frightening and freeing. It is frightening because at some level I feel that I cannot really change my life. After all, I am just a victim of circumstance, aren't I, plugging along with varying degrees of good and bad luck. On the other hand, it is freeing because it may mean that I really do have the ability to make my life better through making myself better and healthier.

I am responsible for my life.

Every therapist knows that the crucial first step in therapy is the patient's assumption of responsibility for his or her life predicament. As long as one believes that one's problems are caused by some force or agency outside oneself, there is no leverage in therapy. If, after all, the problem lies out there, then why should one change oneself? It is the outside world (friends, job, spouse) that must be changed—or exchanged.

Irwin D. Yalom, M.D.

Time

I recognize that there are two concepts of time. There is earth time, by which I structure my day and by which society operates, that is tied to three dimensions of space, time and circumstance and there is timeless time, or that state beyond time of simple beingness. Though I operate by earth time, I need not get stuck there. I always have access to another level of time through the quiet and stillness within me. Each day I will allow myself to be with timeless time.

I will spend time in eternity.

Physicists themselves are not consistent in how they employ these concepts. They may use one set of definitions in the laboratory but lapse back into the ideas of common sense when they leave the job. In spite of these uncertainties, I will refer . . . to two types of time: (1) the time of common sense (linear, flowing, external time; the time of progress, development, and history), and (2) the time that is alluded to in modern physics (nonflowing, nonlinear time; the "time of eternity"; the time in which things do not happen, but simply "are").

Larry Dossey, M.D.

Surrender

I will allow myself to let go and let God today. So much grace and beauty enters my life when I can get out of my own way and let life work out. When, on the other hand, I try to force circumstances to be a certain way, I am unable to be present in them as they are. Each day probably has the potential to work out if I can only let it, if I can learn to move with the natural flow rather than try to control and manipulate the events of my life. Like the weather, my life has a natural rhythm. When I can be in sync with that natural rhythm, things run more smoothly. Today I will have faith, I will trust that if I allow my life to unfold and if I stay present and alive, I will come to understand how to live.

I trust in my ability to live my life well.

God, give us grace to accept with serenity the things that cannot be changed, courage to change the things which should be changed, and the wisdom to distinguish the one from the other.

Reinhold Niebuhr

An Emotion of Extremes

I am willing to love today. Taking the risk to feel, to depend and be depended upon brings up all my fears. I know that when I let myself love, life feels more worthwhile and wonderful. The feelings of vulnerability I experience when I feel love for someone are part of the price I pay for feeling alive and connected. When I set myself up inside for the love experience, even if I lose it, my chances of finding it again are good because love begins with me. If I feel willing to love, I will find people to love and will be able to accept their love in return. Who in this world doesn't want to be around someone who can love them?

I choose to love.

Love is an emotion of extremes. It challenges our patience, our understanding and our resources. It heightens our perceptions, and increases our energy and vitality. It is not for the easily defeated or the quickly disillusioned. If we are determined to be lovers, we shall have to accept and acknowledge our passions. Of course we risk being led into mysterious, uncharted, hazardous places, but we can be assured that our lives will never be dull.

Leo Buscaglia

The Mystical Core

Mysticism is a part of and at the core of all true religion. I needn't leave my religion to seek soul. I need to find the soul in my religion. The inevitable trappings of religion, need not drive me away if I don't feel I have to identify them as exclusively pure and good. Religion, when expressed through people, is subject to the limitations of that person. The core of the religion is still mystical, still concerned with understanding the voice and heart of God and spiritual light. I will listen for the deeper message behind and within the metaphoric lessons of my religion, remembering that the true purpose of religion is to light a path toward soul; to offer touchstones and markers left by those who have traveled the path for others to find their way.

I see the mystery behind the words.

"Every religion has a mystical core," writes Brother David Steindl Rast, a Benedictine monk. . . . "The challenge is to find access to it and to live in its power. In this sense, every generation of believers is challenged anew to make its religion truly religious."

Ronald S. Miller

Barriers

My task in life is to work with myself sincerely and honestly. To remove the emotional and mental obstacles that are in the way of my personal well-being and my soul experience. Soul is, light is; it is what I put in their way that keeps me from experiencing them. My anxiety, depression, sense of meaninglessness and purposelessness can also be seen as loss of soul. By being willing to own and grapple with personal pain, I act on my commitment to deepen my relationship with soul and to open my heart to love. Love and fear are two primary feelings. I can identify with either. Fear is not only fear of another, but fear of my reaction to another—which is fear of myself. I can work with my fear of life, of loneliness, of existential boredom so that I can release them and move through my inner barriers that block my experience of love.

I will work with my inner pain and fear.

Your task is not to seek for love, but merely to seek and find all of the barriers within yourself that you have built against it.

A Course in Miracles

The Mystical Experience

Perhaps we conceive of the mystical experience as being arrived at through a sort of perfect tranquility and peace; but just as or even more frequently, it would appear that this breakthrough into the comprehension of the transcendent nature of life comes through human suffering, through a dark night of the soul.

▼

I can grow spiritually wherever I am.

Love is the ultimate and the highest goal to which man can aspire. Then I grasped the meaning of the greatest secret that human poetry and human thought and belief have to impart: The salvation of man is through love and in love. . . . In a position of utter desolation, when man cannot express himself in positive action, when his only achievement may consist in enduring his sufferings in the right way—an honorable way—in such a position man can, through loving contemplation of the image he carries of his beloved, achieve fulfillment. For the first time in my life I was able to understand the meaning of the words, "The angels are lost in perpetual contemplation of an infinite glory."

Viktor E. Frankl

Matter and the Creative Mind

Nature is filled with such staggering beauty that it is hard for me to think that it just happened by chance. How many artists have set their brushes to trying to re-create on canvas just a corner of the incredible loveliness of a sunset, or a landscape, or just one flower? No matter how skilled the artist, what makes a painting a work of art is felt in the artist's love and interpretation. Today I will cocreate my experience of life with the divine mind.

I tune into the one creative mind.

[Think] God I am Divine Mind—then know definitely that your statement is true and in full accord with Divine Law and Principle. In this way you are fully aware that heaven is all around you. Now is the opportune time to know that all are as free to accomplish this as you are. Now realize that matter was never conceived until thought set it up as a reality. Remember that matter never smiles, neither does it have any power or energy to rule or master itself; it is also devoid of instinct or volition of its own. It is foreign to all other substance.

David T. Spalding

Opening to Receive

I will deepen my ability to receive today, and with it deepen my internal container for life and spirituality. Receiving is also a form of giving. A good receiver returns the gift of giving. How many of us can really receive? Receive the gift of life, health, human love. When I receive these gifts I am able to go through my day feeling full rather than empty. When I open to receive God's love on a daily basis, I am constantly renewed, fed and nurtured. Now feeling full, I have something to give. Now feeling blessed, I can allow others to be blessed and take pleasure in both of our good fortunes. Now understanding what it means to receive, I can live without taking and grabbing. Instead, I make myself a willing and grateful receiver of life and soul.

I open to receive.

Only those who have, receive.

Joseph Roux

December

Withdraw into yourself and look. And if you do not find yourself beautiful yet, act as does the creator of a statue that is to be made beautiful: he cuts away here, he smooths there, he makes this line lighter, this other purer, until a lovely face has grown upon his work. So do you also: cut away all that is excessive, straighten all that is crooked, bring light to all that is overcast, labour to make one glow of beauty and never cease chiselling your statue, until there shall shine out on you from it the godlike splendour of virtue, until you shall see the perfect goodness surely established in the stainless shrine. When you know that you have become this perfect work, when you are self-gathered in the purity of your being, nothing now remaining that can shatter that inner unity, nothing from without clinging to the authentic man, when you find yourself wholly true to your essential nature, wholly that only veritable Light which is not measured by space, not narrowed to any circumscribed form nor again diffused as a thing void of term, but ever unmeasurable as something greater than all measure and more than all quantity—when you perceive that you have grown to this, you are now become the very vision; now call up all your confidence, strike forward yet a step—you need a guide no longer.

Plotinius

Controlling the Outcome

Attempting to control the outcome of events sets me up for disappointment. It solidifies my expectations in only one direction and I miss all the living in between. It makes me want to manage people and events so that they will not do anything that threatens my idea of how things ought to go. When I attempt to manipulate and manage people, I set up a tension in the dynamic between us. I make the event as I see it in my mind more important than the people who are participating in it. I drain myself, others and situations of their spontaneity, which inhibits all of our connections with spirit and soul. Creativity and spontaneity need to flow freely in and out of the reality of time and space, so that they can breathe life and energy onto the stage of life.

I detach from my need to
control the outcome.

There is only one way to happiness and that is to cease worrying about things which are beyond the power of our will.

Epictetus

Saying Yes to Life

My life is up to me. The way I live my life reflects who I am. My love of life and my recognition of the spiritual nature of living begin from a point within me. I am destined to find moral purpose and spiritual meaning in the life I have been given. My decision to live with faith in a higher reality and in my fellow being is an act of both moral courage and child-like innocence. Today I am not worrying about what life can give me, but of what I can give to life. If I am only here to take, I will create a unidirectional black hole within me. Give and take are what keep spirit in natural motion.

I believe in life.

Thinking in mythological terms helps to put you in accord with the inevitables of this vale of tears. You learn to recognize the positive values in what appear to be the negative moments and aspects of your life. The big question is whether you are going to be able to say a hearty yes to your adventure . . . the adventure of the hero—the adventure of being alive.

Joseph Campbell

▼

Intimacy

A loving and intimate relationship is a powerful arena for soul growth. The power of intimacy pulls out of the depths of each person's unconscious—the embedded knots and wounds that long, in the silence of our unconscious, to be recognized and healed. Healthy love in relationships can contain the pain involved in reaching through the lower to the higher self. A loving bond can tolerate struggle and provide a container in which to live and grow.

▼

I respect and cherish the power of intimacy.

Love . . . has the power to unite our disparate parts, to contract or reconstruct our self as we find ourselves meeting another self. . . . Aggressions get rearranged in a trusting intimacy. We fight through to the best truth of each other and what we find we find together and fight together rather than each against the other. Of course, the physical components of love are marvelous. They may be all that can match the wide openness of one body to another that we know as infants with our mothers. Such love, in body as well as soul, in mind as well as heart, will set up a humming that resounds with a simple happiness in being.

Ann and Barry Ulanov

The Opinions of Others

Today I will wear my hat crooked and my buttons wrong. What others may think of me is not my concern—it is entirely up to them, not my business. My business is to experience myself and my life in this alive universe. How can I contact soul if I am worried about how soul will look to others, how I will come off as a person experiencing my soul nature? When I get lost in worrying about what others might think, I spend all my time attempting to manage what I imagine they might be thinking . . . whether they are thinking it or not. I lose contact with my own experience and expend my energy trying to procure or avoid an imagined experience, a feared experience or a wished for experience. The opinions of others can rule me if I let them. Fearing them can rob me of my very direction in life. They can keep me from actualizing my own dreams or living as I might like to live.

The opinions of others belong to them.

Literature is strewn with the wreckage of men who have minded beyond reason the opinions of others.

Virginia Woolf

Social Awareness

I tune in to the creative and spiritual energy that I see and sense in the world today. We are a world in a state of cleansing—walls that once threatened to divide people forever have fallen, repressive nations no longer are viable, the evils that we do to one another are out in the open where their darkness can be bleached by the sun. People's creativity is everywhere in evidence. The spirit of this age seems to me to be changing things on the level of person, city, country and world. Everywhere, people are coming into the awareness of soul and self. I join this call to revolution, this battle against evil fought first in the confines of the heart and next in the world at large. I tune into the positive, unseen forces at work in my day—in my world.

I believe in life.

Who has not the spirit of his age,
Of his age has all the unhappiness.

Voltaire

Slowing Down

I will take my time today. I will slow down and pay attention to what I am doing. When I am constantly rushed and preoccupied, life ceases to make sense to me. My days whiz by me unfelt and unseen. I develop a habit of mind that keeps me ever a little bit elsewhere and away from the moment. Unfortunately, that elsewhere is really nowhere. Being endlessly preoccupied and mentally busy do not mean I get more accomplished. In fact, I accomplish less because I never have my full attention at my disposal. Just by the simple act of slowing down and taking my time, the quality of my life changes. Life is a series of experiences: when the quality of my experience deepens and becomes more enjoyable, so does my life. Today, when I catch myself running here and there in my mind, I will take some deep breaths and relax. I will become more present.

I will take my time.

Slow down and enjoy life. It's not only the scenery you miss by going too fast—you all miss the sense of where you are going and why.

Eddie Cantor

Family Relationships

I will step back and look at what I expect from my family relationships. If my family member were a friend, would I ask the same things that I ask of my family? Do I feel I am entitled to an automatic return "just because they are family," and a lifetime of what I want? Or am I able to see family members as people —people who are not born only to live up to my expectations, people who have their own paths that have little to do with me.

I will examine my expectations.

People would examine *how well they function in some areas of their life and make the equivalent translation to their close family relationships, they would improve their function in the family one hundred percent. Expectations may get the job done but the emotional climate is stifling. Decades from now we will all be dead. What will it matter if the beds were made or unmade. . . . What will matter and influence people long after we are gone is the emotional legacy that we leave to our children and through them to their children. This will have influence on when we are all forgotten.*

Thomas Fogarty, M.D.

Creative Visualization

I will make use of my mind's natural ability to visualize something that I would like to learn or achieve today. I will use my mind to move through my mental blocks toward doing something. Once I know what it is, I will allow myself to see it in my mind; a situation I wish to experience. I will mentally accept it as already happening. I will taste it, feel it, smell it and experience it as if it were really happening; as if it were already a natural part of my life. Then I will let it go just as easily as I would any other thought. Over and over throughout my day, I will allow this image to run through my mind, to see it, feel it and let it go.

I acknowledge my mind's ability to create.

Visualization is the way we think. Before words, images were. . . . The human brain programs and self-programs through its images. Riding a bicycle, driving a car, learning to read, bake a cake, play golf—all skills are acquired through the image-making process. Visualization is the ultimate consciousness tool.

Mike Samuels, M.D., and Nancy Samuels

The Terror of Knowing Soul

Setting soul up as a thing apart divides me from it and can even cause me not to take responsibility for manifesting it in my life. Soul is not something that I visit one day a week—it is with me all the time. It is an allowing, a recognition, a point of view, alive and a part of all that exists. Soul cannot solve my problems for me. I do not reach it once and for all and stay there. It will not make me rich or famous; it is not a sabbatical from living. Soul is frighteningly simple and terrifyingly complex, close at hand and out of reach, the center of my existence and yet a mystery.

I can live with the intensity of being awake.

Instead of being at the mercy of wild beasts, earth-quakes, landslides, and inundations, modern man is battered by the elemental forces of his own psyche. This is the World Power that vastly exceeds all other powers on earth. The Age of Enlightenment, which stripped nature and human institutions of gods, overlooked the God of Terror who dwells in the human soul.

Carl Jung

375

▼

Relationships

I will examine myself today. The way that I act is a reflection of who I am. If I really wish to know myself. I will observe myself in action. My behavior doesn't come out of nowhere; if I study it, it can tell me how I think. Relationships call forward deep parts of myself, they ask me to respond spontaneously over and over again. My spontaneous reactions are the best indicator of who I am inside—through them I come to know myself. How am I with people, what kind of relationships do I have in my life and how do I act within them? Am I able to be intimate—do I move in too close or out too far? Where do I place myself vis-á-vis others in my life?

▼

I look at the relationships in my life.

Only in relationships can you know yourself, not in abstraction and certainly not in isolation. The movement of behavior is the sure guide to yourself, it's the mirror of your consciousness; this mirror will reveal its content, the images, the attachments, the fears, the loneliness, the joy and sorrow. Poverty lies in running away from this, either in its sublimating or its identities.

Jiddu Krishnamurti

The Existence of Soul

I will assume that soul exists, whatever soul is, whether it be personal, corporal or ethereal, my own or belonging to a collective. I will take it for granted. If trees and sky and air and birds are real, then how can they not be alive and laced with spirit? If I can think these thoughts and feel these feelings, then soul is alive in me, guiding my inner workings and my outer movements.

I assume the existence of soul.

We have now discovered that it was an intellectually unjustified presumption on our forefathers' part to assume that Man has a Soul . . . that there is a power inherent in it which builds up the body, supports its life, heals its ills and enables the soul to live independently of the body . . . and that beyond our empirical present, there is a spiritual world from which the soul receives knowledge of spiritual things whose origins cannot be discovered in this physical world. But . . . it is just as presumptuous and fantastic for us to assume that matter produces spirit.

Carl Jung

The One Reality

Today, rather than seek soul in the extraordinary, I will learn to identify it in every ordinary activity I perform. I will seek contact and connection with soul energy in whatever I think, feel or do. Instead of allowing thought, emotion and activity to divide me from soul, I will let it unite me. I will use my faculties to lead me toward rather than away from spirit. I will look for direct contact with the energy that breathes life into this universe, this world in which I live. If I am alive, I am one with all that is alive. It is simply a matter of coming into consciousness of this truth, of waking up. If the Berlin wall can fall, then the wall dividing me from my higher self can fall as well.

I wake up to the truth.

The criterion of mental health is not one of individual adjustment to a given social order, but a universal one, valid for all men, of giving a satisfactory answer to the problem of human existence.

Erich Fromm

Creative Expression

Creativity is alive and well in my home today. It is evidenced in the extra attention I pay to the arrangement of a shelf or table top, to the food that I cook or the way that I present it. Creativity is a part of the activities that I choose to undertake and the way that I enjoy them. It is bringing a fresh eye to an ordinary day. Children are creative, and being with them unblocks my spontaneity—it challenges me to stay present in the moment. The work that I do is creative not necessarily because of the nature of it, but because of the way I approach it. Approaching my life with a creative spirit actually gives me energy. It entices me to dig my hands deep into the stuff of life, work with it and make it my own. My creative spirit propels me to move ever energetically into the next challenge. It brings me closer to the creative spirit that breathes life into this world.

I look with an artist's eye.

The creative person is both more primitive and more cultivated, more destructive, a lot madder and a lot saner, than the average person.

Frank Barron

A Pathless Land

I will not look for access to my own soul through dogma or through other people's experiences. I will rely on my own experience instead. Soul is not a path or a place. It is an experience. I enter it through the door of self and I rest there both lost and found, serene and stimulated, satisfied and challenged. When the illusion of three-dimensional reality falls away and I see the world for the alive, luminous and vibrating reality that it is, then I stop searching and start having, I stop wandering and start being. Soul is an experience waiting to happen. It starts to happen when I let it, right here, right now—this moment.

I invite soul into this moment.

I maintain that Truth is a pathless land, and you cannot approach it by any path whatsoever, by any religion, by any sect.

Jiddu Krishnamurti

Listening to my Creativity

I will listen carefully to my inner voice. I am entitled to a meaningful work in life. Aligning myself with the creative energy within and without me aligns me with the process of living, of giving birth to something, nurturing and sustaining, helping something to grow toward fruition. Holding myself back from moving forward into life with creative energy is a sort of deprivation. It keeps me from engaging in life and enjoying a sense of excitement and accomplishment. To create something, whether it be a meal, a book or a business, is deeply satisfying.

I allow myself to be creative.

It is all a question of sensitiveness. Brute force and overbearing may make a terrific effect. But in the end, that which lives, lives by delicate sensitiveness. If it were a question of brute force, not a single human baby would survive for a fortnight. It is the grass of the field, most frail of all things, that supports all life all the time. But for the green grass, no empire would rise, no man would eat bread: for grain is grass; and Hercules or Napoleon or Henry Ford would alike be denied existence.

D. H. Lawrence

Separating the Past from the Present

I can separate my past from my present. When I over-react to a present-day circumstance, when I bring reactivity or judgment that is out of sync with what is really happening, I will back up and ask myself why. What has this present-day circumstance triggered in me, what feelings has it brought up that are not really about what is happening now, but more about what has happened? I will use my over-reactions today as indications of where I have unfinished business and unresolved emotions. What is the person or situation from my past that I still carry unresolved pain from? When I make this connection, I will feel the feelings surrounding the *original* situation, so that they do not continually get played out in my present.

I am alerted to unfinished business.

Respect the past in the full measure of its deserts, but do not make the mistake of confusing it with the present nor seek it in the ideals of the future.

José Ingenieros

Madness

I will use my craziness to lead me into more of me, more of self and soul. Whatever is driving me mad needs looking at. It is an indicator of my own unfinished business. If it were not, my response would be less intense, less overwhelming. Only a few circumstances in life legitimately drive me mad. When this happens I will take time with my self, I will pay closer attention to what is going on with me. Rather than seeing my feelings as only a reaction to another person or situation, I will accept them as my own. I will sit with them and pay attention to what arises within me. I will make a sincere effort to own what is mine, knowing that the more of me I am truly and honestly connected with, the more of me I am willing to hold and claim, the more I will have room for soul.

▼

I own what is mine.

Madness need not be all breakdown. It may also be break-through. It is potential liberation and renewal as well as enslavement and existential death.

R. D. Laing

▼

Learning

Sitting in stillness brings up old wounds. It makes the fears and anxieties that I carry daily more present. Part of my path toward soul will be a sort of unlearning. When I was a child, I came to emotional conclusions that were based on the way a child thinks and perceives. Oftentimes as a child, I felt powerless, as if I were at the beck and call of the adults in my life—subject to their whims. Other times I felt powerful, as if I alone were responsible for a situation. As an adult, I understand that neither of these positions is accurate.

▼

I look at what I learned.

Individual brain cells, after repeated exposure to similar events, begin to react in the same fashion each time: In other words, they learn. The human brain then starts to categorize and (to) group images, and then we use these complex sets to make abstractions. This process, created and reinforced in childhood, creates memories, which rarely go away. They may be hidden from the conscious mind, but they remain locked in the brain, waiting for a trigger to bring them to the surface.

Daniel Akron

▼

Worry and Strain

Often I try to solve a problem by adding more information. When that does not solve it, I seek out more. The more my search yields nothing, the more desperate I become for just the right answer, the correct word or phrase that will dispel all my anxiety and solve the ache in my heart—forever. There are no answers—there is only the quiet speaking to me, the void reaching out its hand for me to take. The answer, if there is one, emerges in the stillness within one or reveals itself naturally over time. I do not need to feel afraid of falling into a dark abyss within my soul. I do not need to be afraid because God is there. There is no reality that is not penetrated by God.

▼

I am alive.

If we did not worry, most of us would feel we were not alive. To be struggling with a problem is for the majority of us an indication of existence. We cannot imagine life without a problem; and the more we are occupied with a problem, the more alert we think we are. . . . Will worry resolve the problem or does the answer . . . come when the mind is quiet?

Jiddu Krishnamurti

Doing and Growing

Trying to have purity of life, soul and spirit automatically is like the fantasy of flying over traffic; it just doesn't work that way. In order to have results, I need to be willing to put in the time. It is when I am willing to do my part and participate that I learn and grow by doing. My lessons and rewards are waiting for me—I just need to be willing to participate, here on earth, where I live. Soul and life are manifested through action. Today I will be in my day.

I engage in my surroundings.

But those rare souls whose spirit gets magically into the hearts of men, leave behind them something more real and warmly personal than bodily presence, an ineffable and eternal thing. It is everlasting life touching us as something more than a vague, recondite concept. The sound of a great name dies like an echo; the splendor of fame fades into nothing; but the grace of a fine spirit pervades the places through which it has passed, like the haunting loveliness of mignonettes.

Phil Cousineau

Simple Living

Life has taught me not to grasp and hold, but to stand with a flat empty hand and allow the flow to happen. What is unfolding itself to me right now is enough. By aligning myself with this energy I remain amused, fed and delighted by life. Deciding ahead what will make me happy and waiting for that to manifest before I allow myself to experience happiness is missing the point. Happiness is in the seeing and the experiencing. Happiness is a simple thing—it comes from living life rather than planning to live life. Life is not a rehearsal, it is what is happening *right now*.

I experience the simplicity of life.

May all beings everywhere plagued with sufferings of body and mind quickly be freed from their illnesses. May those frightened cease to be afraid, and may those bound be free. May the powerless find power, and may people think of befriending one another. May those who find themselves in trackless, fearful wildernesses—the children, the aged, the unprotected—be guarded by beneficent celestials, and may they swiftly attain Buddhahood.

Buddhist prayer

Balancing the Inner and Outer World

I will worry less about fitting in with the world and more about fitting the world in with me. When I was a child, I allowed my inner world to shine through; in growing up I grew away from my own insides. I split off from my own inner being and put my energy into matching myself with what I saw around me, whether or not it was in accord with who I was, my own particular likes and dislikes. Eventually, I lost contact with what I really thought and felt and became dependent on others to tell me about myself. I looked to others for confirmation and affirmation because I had silenced my own inner voice.

I will listen to my own insides.

Remember that you ought to behave in life as you would at a banquet. As something is being passed around it comes to you; stretch out your hand, take a portion of it politely. It passes on; do not detain it. Or it has not come to you yet; do not project your desire to meet it, but wait until it comes in front of you. So act toward children, so toward a wife, so toward office, so toward wealth.

Epictetus

Seeing Through Things

Today I will look through rather than at. The situations and circumstance of this world are to some extent contrived, and the people within them are playing roles. When I mistake the circumstance and the roles being played for ultimate truth, when I take them so seriously that I can't see beyond them, I spend my time reacting. Though I play roles, it is important for me to remember that I am not my roles. Though the world seems to be the last word on reality, I will remind myself that it is only a play, a scene. I need not take it so seriously, allowing it to make me nervous and anxious. I already belong to a larger, more important life—the world of the soul.

I see through and beyond the surface.

May there be peace on earth. May the waters be appeasing. May herbs be wholesome, and may trees and plants bring peace to all. May all beneficent beings bring peace to us. . . . May the Vedic Law propagate peace all through the world. May all things be a source of peace to us. And may peace itself, bestow peace on all, and may that peace come to me also.

Hindu prayer

Accomplishment

I do not need to move mountains in order to experience a sense of accomplishment. I only need to keep my mind clear and my goals well grounded. There is nothing like a true feeling of accomplishing real day-to-day objectives to produce a sense of well-being and eliminate the need for grandiosity. Genuine accomplishment is its own reward, the good feeling it produces makes life worth living. Genuine accomplishment allows the energies of soul to flow through me and find expression in simple, real ways. If I can only experience accomplishment when I overachieve, I will miss the beauty of what a sense of accomplishment is all about. When I put my heart into my actions and perform the duties of my life with love and devotion, I move closer to soul.

I take pleasure in simple
daily accomplishments.

Let a human being through the energies of his soul into the making of something, and the instinct of workmanship will take care of his honesty.

Walter Lippmann

Doing My Part

I will do my part. Pointing my finger at society and blaming it, displacing personal responsibility onto the powers that be, will not help me or anyone else. Rather, I will do what I can to help. The world needs me more than ever. I can and will make a difference. If all that I accomplish is to not make matters worse, it will be enough. What have I to lose by trying? I lose my soul when I give up on life because soul and life travel on the same wind. If I love and value one, I love and value the other. I will stretch my arm out in front of me and all around. I will pay attention to what is within my sphere of influence. If I choose soul then I choose the world as well.

I choose to value life.

The truth is, young people are not saved by bureaucrats sitting behind desks in Washington, DC, or, for that matter, Atlanta, Georgia. They're saved one at a time by people like you, by volunteers in churches and boys clubs, and by teachers and coaches in schools. And most importantly, they're saved at home. Abraham Lincoln said it simply, "The hand that rocks the cradle rules the world."

James O. Mason, Assistant Secretary for Health, 1991

▼

Living History

I will come to understand the beauty of the life that is lived within my mind and heart. It is not what surrounds me, but how I experience, process and contain what surrounds me that gives my life its personal meaning and purpose. When I have to let go of one stage of life and move into another, I do not need to lose the beauty of that time—I can re-experience it within me again and again, savoring and enjoying it whenever I wish for it, whenever I need it, whenever someone else wants access to it through me.

▼

I will share my story.

Never have I enjoyed youth so thoroughly as I have in my old age. In writing Dialogues in Limbo, The Last Puritan, *and now all these descriptions of the friends of my youth and the young friends of my middle age, I have drunk the pleasure of life more pure, more joyful than it ever was when mingled with all the hidden anxieties and little annoyances of actual living. Nothing is inherently and invincibly young except spirit. And spirit can enter a human being perhaps better in the quiet of old age and dwell there more undisturbed than in the turmoil of adventure.*

George Santayana

Believing in Love

Today I will take one more step toward soul and toward love. That step may be to take a risk, to move from my inner path what blocks me, to resolve a conflict or to attempt to be honest in a relationship. Whatever attempt I make, I will not judge myself for my awkwardness. If my heart is sincere, I will know that God is smiling on me no matter how inept I feel. But growth is messy. If I want to look good and never put my foot in my mouth or look like a fool, I will have to maintain the status quo. The risk of growth is the risk of creating a mess as a part of healing and growing. Each little step I take is worthwhile if my heart is in it. I will not judge myself by the mess. I will judge myself by my sincere desire to grow. What I don't have, I can't give away.

I will learn.

To be a child . . . is to have a spirit yet streaming from the waters of baptism; it is to believe in love, to believe in loveliness, to believe in belief . . . lowness into loftiness, and nothing into everything, for each child has its fairy godmother in its soul.

Francis Thompson

Normal Day

I treasure this day. I love it because it is ordinary. My uneventful, business-as-usual day is for me like a quiet, well-crafted tune that I can listen to over and over again. The easy and natural things of life give me deep pleasure today. I am aware of what a gift life is—to inhabit this body is a privilege. The human and the divine meet in this simple moment, this ordinary day. There is a quiet majesty in its simplicity. There is nothing missing. There is a spirit that lives in this day, it speaks through the mind and grows upward through the ground, it casts warmth and fragrance and sunlight.

I do not need overflow to feel alive.

Normal day, let me be aware of the treasure you are. Let me learn from you, love you, savor you, bless you before you depart. Let me not pass you by in quest of some rare and perfect tomorrow. Let me hold you while I may for it will not always be so. One day I shall dig my nails into the earth, or bury my face in the pillow, or stretch myself taut, or raise my hands to the sky, and want, more than all the world, your return.

Mary Jean Irion

Lighting One Candle

I will do what I can today. My contribution to society may not earn me a Nobel Prize or fame or wealth, but it is what I have to give. Why should I hold back my contribution because I don't feel it is as worthy or significant as another person's? Though someone else may have seemingly more to give, it is simply what *they* have to offer. Let them give it and let me contribute in my own way. Every sensitive generous act is worthy. Sometimes the sweetest gifts are smiling at someone who feels forgotten or listening to a person who is in pain. These are gifts of the spirit, of the self, and they are significant. When I give of myself, I give something everlasting—something that can be carried in the heart and spirit of another person something that cannot be destroyed by the elements. I give a piece of eternity.

I will give what I can.

It is better to light one candle than curse the darkness.

Christopher Society motto, the sentiment
of which is an old Chinese proverb

A Sacred Place

I will keep a sacred place in my life and in my day. I will hold out time to be, time to allow my soul to emerge into the now, into my world and my life. As good as I may be at understanding or thinking about soul, my life will only transform with direct experience. When I give myself quiet time, I am inviting soul's energy to manifest in my day. This is how I will come to understand the true meaning of soul—not through thinking but through being, not through chasing but through sitting.

I enter the discipline of soul awareness.

A sacred place is an absolute necessity for anybody today. You must have a room or a certain hour of the day when you don't know what was in the newspaper that morning. You don't know who your friends are, you don't know what you owe to anybody . . . but a place where you can simply bring forth what you are or what you might be. This is a place of creative incubation. At first you may find that nothing's happening there. But if you have a sacred place and you use it and you take advantage of it . . . something will happen.

Joseph Campbell

The Energy of Love

Today I will trust the power that lies within the energy of love. Where intelligence and wealth will fail, love will find a way. It is through love that I forgive and forget, that I reach beyond myself to put aside my anger, resentment and greed because the love I feel recognizes that there is a better way. Love gives meaning, order and beauty to my life. It creates meaning in what could be seen as an otherwise boring, banal life. Love leads me gently toward my higher self and toward the higher selves of others. Love spurs me on to look past the surface toward what might be better in myself, in my world and in other people. Love is both the tie that binds and the energy that frees. Love prepares me for the soul experience.

Love and soul are one.

The day will come when, after harnessing the ether, the winds, the tides, gravitation, we shall harness for God the energies of love. And, on that day, for the second time in the history of the world, man will have discovered fire.

Pierre Teilhard de Chardin

ABOUT THE AUTHOR

Tian Dayton, Ph.D. in clinical psychology and M.A. in educational psychology, is a therapist in New York City and director of Innerlook, Inc. She is a certified psychodramatist and a consultant at ONSITE, Caron Foundation and the Institute for Sociotherapy.

Tian Dayton's work includes seminal development in the field of psychodrama, training for senior-level health professionals, and workshop presentations both for the public and for the therapeutic community. She is the author of several books appropriate for the lay reader and for the healing professional. These include *The Quiet Voice of Soul, The Drama Within, Drama Games, Keeping Love Alive, Daily Affirmations for Forgiving and Moving On* and *Daily Affirmations for Parents*.

If you would like to obtain information about workshops on soul issues and/or psychodrama across the United States, please send your name, address and phone number to:

Tian Dayton, Ph.D.
Innerlook, Inc.
262 Central Park West
Suite 4A
New York, NY 10024

Affirming Books by *Tian Dayton*

Keeping Love Alive
Inspirations for Commitment

Ideas for appreciating differences, honoring uniqueness and allowing space between two people who love each other.

Code 2603
(5¹/₂ x 7, 128 pp.) $7.95

Daily Affirmations for Forgiving and Moving On
Powerful Inspiration for Personal Change

This book offers positive affirmations of hope, strength and inspiration to help you move on.

Code 2158
(4 x 6, 365 pp.) $7.95

Daily Affirmations for Parents
How to Nurture Your Children and Renew Yourself During the Ups and Downs of Parenthood

This book will guide you through the trials and tribulations of parenthood.

Code 1518
(4 x 6, 366 pp.) $6.95

Available at your favorite bookstore or call 1-800-441-5569 for Visa or MasterCard orders. Prices do not include shipping and handling. Your response code is HCI.

Soul Issues and Psychodrama
by *Tian Dayton*

The Quiet Voice of Soul
How to Find Meaning in Ordinary Life

Dr. Dayton opens our eyes to the many truths and expressions of soul—through family, relationships, feelings, play, the universe and spirituality. The thought-provoking quotes, illustrative vignettes and practical exercises in this marvelous book will serve as your road map to a more meaningful life.
Code 3391
(5½ x 8½, 245 pp.) $9.95

The Drama Within
Psychodrama and Experiential Therapy

Dr. Dayton, a highly respected practitioner of psychodrama within the addictions field, brings together a complete explanation of the theory and practice of psychodrama, directions for specific drama games and methods for applying the theory and games in the treatment of trauma and addiction.
Code 2964
(6 x 9, 291 pp.) $14.95

Drama Games
Techniques for Self-Development

This book is designed to help participants get in touch with and express buried feelings in a safe and structured way and to offer training in the ability to be creative and spontaneous.
Code 021X
(6 x 9, 223 pp.) $7.95

Available at your favorite bookstore or call 1-800-441-5569 for Visa or MasterCard orders. Prices do not include shipping and handling. Your response code is HCI.

Affirm Your Life with
Chicken Soup for the Soul

Chicken Soup for the Soul
101 Stories to Open the Heart
and Rekindle the Spirit
Jack Canfield and Mark Victor Hansen

Code 262X paperback $12.95
Code 2913 hard cover $24.00
Code 3812 large print $16.95

A 2nd Helping of
Chicken Soup for the Soul
101 More Stories to Open the Heart
and Rekindle the Spirit
Jack Canfield and Mark Victor Hansen

Code 3316 paperback $12.95
Code 3324 hard cover $24.00
Code 3820 large print $16.95

Chicken Soup for the Soul Cookbook
Stories and Recipes from the Heart
Jack Canfield, Mark Victor Hansen and
Diana von Welanetz Wentworth

Code 3545 paperback $16.95
Code 3634 hard cover $29.95

A 3rd Serving of
Chicken Soup for the Soul
101 More Stories to Open the Heart
and Rekindle the Spirit
Jack Canfield and Mark Victor Hansen

Code 3790 paperback $12.95
Code 3804 hard cover $24.00